What You
Can Do with
a Horse

What You
Can Do with
a Horse

Sally Stull

South Brunswick
New York: A. S. Barnes and Company
London: Thomas Yoseloff Ltd

A. S. Barnes and Co., Inc.
Cranbury, New Jersey 08512

Thomas Yoseloff Ltd
Magdalen House
136-148 Tooley Street
London SE1 2TT, England

Library of Congress Cataloging in Publication Data

Stull, Sally.
What you can do with a horse.

Includes index.
1. Horses. 2. Horsemanship. I. Title.
SF285.S925   798'.23   75-38439
ISBN 0-498-01786-9

Printed in the United States of America

To Heather,
for whose tomorrows
this book was written

Contents

Preface

If you want to find out "where the action is" within the horse industry, join a club. Which club? Well, just take your pick!

Organizations of all kinds exist for all sorts of equestrian purposes. Some groups promote fancy show-horse breeds, and some dedicate themselves to the salvation of wild mustangs. Others focus on teaching equitation skills, and still others emphasize horse management. Groups exist to hunt foxes, and groups also exist to hunt the hunters.

What You Can Do with a Horse is an introductory guidebook to the wide variety of sports and activities available to you within the horse world. No attempt has been made to cover all the bases, and apologies are offered to those organizations and institutions that are not mentioned.

Here is just a glimpse of the many opportunities you'll find. Horses are truly an industry in the United States today, an industry with real financial, emotional, and physical clout. As such, a varied and fascinating subculture has been formed by horse people as they've sought unity among their many purposes and interests.

Newcomers to the horse world, and old-timers who want to stretch their muscles a little, can read the book as a whole. A closer look at chapters of special personal interest can help you blaze a new trail, or clear an old one.

So gobble or taste, as the mood and the need suit you. If I'd known what I do now about the horse world when I was fifteen, I'd probably be pushing a currycomb instead of pounding a typewriter today.

Acknowledgments

Credit for the bulk of this book should go to the people at the many national horse organizations who were so cooperative in providing both informative literature and photographs.

Special thanks also go to Mr. W. Fauntleroy Pursley, Master of Fox Hounds for the Iroquois Hunt in Lexington, Kentucky, for his help with the chapter on hunting. Thanks to Bob and Cathie Toothman of Toothman Stables, South Point, Ohio, for use of their facilities, students, and horses for photo sessions. And thanks to Mrs. Ann Rice of Buena Vista Stables near Ashland, Kentucky, for saddle club information; and to Mrs. Carol Mangione of the Keeneland Pony Club in Lexington for Pony Club help.

What You
Can Do with
a Horse

Horse racing is the mainstay of the entire horse industry; more people go to the races than to all the pro ball games put together! Horse races generate emotion, and horse racing generates money—millions of dollars each year. *Courtesy Keeneland Association.*

1

Horses Are Everybody's Business

Are you a horse nut? Well, look around you—the horse is back. And as is said of a legendary superhero, "He's everywhere, he's everywhere!"

From suburban stables to gigantic urban racing complexes, horses are on the American scene to stay. Their number has at least tripled in the last fifteen years as horse fever has grown by leaps and bounds.

The U.S. Department of Agriculture estimates that horse racing alone draws more people than any other spectator sport in the country. Nearly as many fans turn out for the races as attend pro and college football and major and minor league baseball!

Dollar signs and horses go hand in hoof. Racing generates close to *five billion dollars* every year, and produces close to half a million dollars in state and local taxes.

The race horse population by itself is growing at the rate of fifteen percent a year. In New York, thirty thousand people earn at least half their incomes from track-associated activities. Racing means money off-track, too: the value of race-horse breeding farms runs into billions of dollars. Several syndicated studs are valued at over one million dollars—remember Secretariat?—and breeding fees are set at thousands of dollars.

Undoubtedly, horses make more money racing than they do at anything, and probably everything, else. But most of our horses are used for fun, and so a big chunk of the horse world belongs to the little guy—to you and to me. For according to the National Horse and Pony Youth Activities Council, three million families keep eight million horses on two million acres of land—with an annual financial impact of over thirteen billion dollars!

We've made horses big business. And although some of our animals still work for a living, most have come a long way from pulling carriages and hauling freight to earn their hay.

15

Individual owners put in their share of money, right along with the big guys. The USDA figures that after a person buys a horse—be it plug pony or spirited show animal—he or she spends from $250 to $2,000 a year on each horse, for feed, shelter, tack, drugs, and the like. In addition, no other class of livestock pays as much money to the government in taxes as do horses and horse people.

All kinds of horse activity have come to be grouped together under the common term *the horse industry*. And with good reason.

As we've seen, millions of horses naturally mean billions of dollars worth of business, not only to agriculture, where horses are gobbling up record amounts of hay and grain, but to our national economy as well. In fact, the horse industry has become such big business that a specialized trade organization exists in Washington to look after horsemen's Congressional interests.

The American Horse Council represents more than seventy horse organizations and two million individual horse people. Formed in 1969, the AHC lobbies for the entire industry when horse-related legislation comes up in Congress. The Council encourages cooperation between the horse industry and government, helps to ensure continued government funding for research programs, and in general provides a legislative liaison between horse people and their Congressmen.

Within the government structure, the USDA Extension Service stays alert to the needs of horsemen through its new Horse Industry Advisory Council. The HIAC is concerned with horse industry studies, horse censuses, development of riding trails on public lands, disease control, etc. The group was set up on the recommendation of the American Horse Council, and it advises the Department of Agriculture on specialized horse industry needs.

To a lot of Americans, then, horses mean bread and butter. But while horses help line pockets all over the country, the owners of those pockets understand that perhaps the horse's greatest influence isn't financial at all. The spiritual and emotional experience of owning a horse, or just being around one, has no equal.

Most encouraging to adult horse lovers is the place horses have taken in the hearts of young people. You might say that teenagers are taking over the horse world.

More than half a million young people belong to horse organizations in the United States today. Nearly 225,000 affiliate with 4-H Light Horse and Pony Clubs, in a membership that increases by twenty thousand each year! Half the members of the influential American Horse Shows Association are under eighteen. Then you have the junior-division members of national horse breed associations, the Future Farmers, the Boy and Girl Scout mounted troops.

Rodeo is a way of life for all sorts of people, riders and spectators alike. All kinds of organizations exist for rodeo promotion at various levels—competition starts in earnest at age eight! *Courtesy International Rodeo Association.*

No matter where you live, there's probably at least one horse show within fifty miles of you almost every summer weekend. Nearly three thousand shows are sanctioned by one group or another, as are almost one thousand rodeos. Thousands more operate locally.

Thank the young people here, too. Horse shows are virtually dominated by young entries. By sheer force of numbers, junior horse people have swelled the entries lists so that bigger and better shows are always in the making. Rodeo associations now entice youngsters as young as eight and on up through high school and college. Rodeo has become a recognized intramural sport at many Western schools.

As young people become involved with horses, they begin to seek permanent places for themselves within the horse industry. The possibilities are endless. Some may choose the rigors of veterinary practice, or of equine research. Still others strive to maintain the arts of blacksmithing and saddlemaking. Some dream of the day when they'll own their own riding school, or training stable, or breeding farm.

The industry has begun to sit up and take notice. Because young people own so many horses, they're naturally a ready market for adequate stabling facilities, professional training, good feed and equipment, and the like, to say nothing of the demand for horses suitable for youth shows and pleasure riding. Most important of all, young horse people are the future of the industry itself.

Consequently, many breed associations have begun to form separate junior associations for their younger members. By encouraging youth to favor their particular breed, these groups have discovered a fail-safe method of continuing their particular breed's popularity. After all, a confirmed young Quarter Horse fancier isn't likely to switch breeds in mid-life!

These adults grew up with horses themselves, and they know the value of horse ownership in growing up. The knowledge gained, the responsibility shouldered, the social experience pop up in life far beyond the confines of a riding arena.

Horses are character builders. Enthusiasts seem to take on responsibility for self and mount in stride. Good horsemanship and practical horse management require and receive a dedication most teens would shudder to apply to their schoolwork. And good sportsmanship just seems to come naturally among people with the same strong concern.

Opportunities for healthy competition abound. Junior horse clubs have awards for different levels of achievement; even nonhorse groups like the Scouts offer merit badges in horsemanship. And there's nothing quite like a first-place blue ribbon—or even a sixth-place green!—to

Steeplechasing—a race over fences—is a horse sport of worldwide popularity. Here riders run for the wire at the Fairyhouse Races in Ireland. *Courtesy Irish Tourist Board.*

bolster the old ego. Some horse clubs even offer scholarships allowing outstanding juniors to further their academic education.

Horses, then, are here to stay. And so are the young people devoted to them. Together they generate tax revenues, stimulate related businesses, serve agriculture, and help to meet our growing recreational needs.

This all goes to prove the worth of an old (if somewhat embellished) adage: The outside of a horse is indeed good for the inside of almost everyone.

And we've only just begun!

2
Let's Go Riding!

When I was a kid I had a secret method, just between me and myself, of finding out if I was *really* sick. I'd ask myself a very simple question: "If you had the chance to go out riding right now, would you feel like it?" No matter what information I'd been putting out to the general public, the secret answer was almost always the same: "Yes! Of course!"

Horse fever hits hard—and young. I know. The affliction is usually severe, and is likely to be terminal (lasting until you die). Girls are more prone than boys, but boys are susceptible, too. The prime symptom is complete inability to turn down the invitation, "Let's go riding!"

Of course, people who own their own horses have no real problem. They can just toddle out to the barn and climb aboard (unless the barn is miles away from home—but that's another story). Most people, however, particularly those who've just come down with horse fever, are faced with the almost constant problem of what and where to ride.

Riding establishments have popped up everywhere in a sometimes desperate attempt to keep pace with the horse's rising popularity. And just as horses themselves come in all sizes, colors, shapes, tempers, and conditions, so do the places we go to ride them.

Someone whose main interest is in vaulting on a horse and taking off for the wild blue yonder shouldn't have much trouble finding his way there. But the serious rider, at whatever level of skill, ought to consider a bit before plunking down good money for lessons.

Study yourself, for instance. What do you really want from horses? From riding? Study the stables in your area. The better the match you can make, the better your chances are for success as a horseman or horsewoman.

One of the most basic concerns of the beginning rider is style. Are you more interested in English or Western riding? Hunt seat, saddle seat, or balance seat? Do you know what the terms mean?

Western horsemanship. Seated in a heavy and comfortable stock saddle, the rider holds reins in one hand and wears relatively long stirrup leathers.

Fundamental differences between English and Western riding styles are most obvious in equipment. Western riders use a large, heavy saddle with a horn in front; English riders use different kinds of flat saddles with metal stirrups. Generally speaking, Western riders hold their reins in one hand, and English riders use both hands.

But reins and stirrups are hardly the most important consideration. What you want to do on a horse will influence the type of equipment you use.

The English saddle in one variation is used for hunting and jumping, and in another guise for showing horses like the Tennessee Walker and the American Saddlebred. It allows a close feel with the horse.

Western saddles open up riding activity to include reining and roping. These big saddles are generally more comfortable over longer periods of time, and they tend to give the rider a feeling of greater security.

Shelves of books have been written on riding styles; I won't go into the fundamentals of horsemanship here. Two especially good treatments of the subject, though, are *Saddle Up! The Farm Journal Book of Western Horsemanship,* written by Charles Bell and published by Lippincott; and *Heads Up, Heels Down,* about English horsemanship, written by C. W. Anderson and published by Macmillan. *Ride American* by Louis Taylor (Harper & Row) covers both styles well in one volume.

So before you can start looking for a good place to ride, you have to take a good look at yourself. You should know how and why you want to ride—or at the very least, what your choices are. And you should think about where all this will lead you eventually. Do you want to compete in horse shows? Are you just interested in learning to ride well enough to enjoy yourself? Do you want to learn horse management so you can someday care for your own animal? Or what? Your purpose will influence your choice of place.

Establishments dealing with riding horses go under many different names: riding academy, school of horsemanship, riding stable, horse center, horses for rent. You can look them up in the phone book. Better yet, talk to someone who's involved in the kind of riding you want to learn. If you don't know anyone, go to a local horse show, find a friendly soul who's doing what you want to do, and ask him where he's learned. You can check, too, at retail stores selling riding clothes and horse equipment.

Whatever a riding school calls itself, it should meet certain minimum standards. And while you're by no means an expert on such things—if you were, would you need a school?—there are ways you can tell whether a particular establishment is apt to be able to teach what it preaches.

Hunt seat equitation. Notice the short stirrups, the English or "flat" saddle, and the rider's special hunt cap and boots.

First of all, check out the grounds. Does anyone really care about the place? Does the sign hang straight? Are the fence boards in place? What about the condition of the riding ring? And how about the stalls where the horses live?

Next, look at the animals themselves. While they probably won't look as fat and sassy as those you see in the show ring, you shouldn't be able to see *all* the ribs. And you should be able to detect some signs of life in the horses' eyes.

Now consider the tack—the saddles and bridles. Are they clean and soft, without ugly cracks in the leather? People who care about horses usually take good care of their equipment, too.

Last and most important, consider the instructors, for on these people much of your own progress and success with riding will depend. A personality conflict with any teacher makes learning anything just that much harder, and learning something fun with someone you don't like just sort of spoils the whole thing.

So you should try to match yourself with an instructor as well as with a stable. Both should be qualified to teach you what you want to learn. But people-watching is more complicated than place-matching. It may take you a little longer to find out what kind of teaching does you the most good, for instance. Some riders want their instructors to come down hard on their mistakes; others prefer a gentler hint.

What makes a good riding instructor? Well, basically, love of horses and love of people, in almost equal amounts. In this country there's no standardized test for riding teachers like there is in England, but we still have a lot of good people. They're just a little harder to find.

A qualified instructor can have any one of a number of different backgrounds. He or she may have made a name in the show ring, or be the veteran of years of teaching experience. You may have the good fortune of running into a graduate of one of the career-oriented horsemanship schools (more on these in chapters 11 and 12); or you may fall into the equally capable hands of a graduate of the School of Hard Knocks.

If a riding school advertises itself as an elected "Riding Establishment Member" of the American Horse Shows Association, then you've hit the jackpot—the AAA of the horse world. Both the facilities and the teachers will be topnotch. (For a current listing of these members see Appendix I.)

Not everybody, however, is blessed with a Riding Establishment Member in the backyard. Many areas of the country, in fact, have no real riding stables at all. Then you have a problem.

Saddle seat equitation. Although casually dressed, this young rider and her horse demonstrate the most formal of riding styles. Note the double reins and special cutback saddle. These riders are taught to keep their hands up, not down; stirrups are worn long.

One of the best solutions seems to be to go to a locally organized horse show and let it be known that you're looking for riding instruction. And that you're willing to pay for the privilege. You may discover a teaching stable that feels no need to advertise but thrives instead on word-of-mouth recommendations. Or you may meet up with an excellent rider who'd like both the teaching experience and the extra pocket money.

A word here about riding-lesson charges. Since today's inflation is moving faster than a race horse, I hesitate to mention figures. Prices vary, of course, from one area to the next, and even from one stable to the next. I think you could safely say, though, that it costs about three dollars to five dollars to ride a horse for an hour without instruction, and from four dollars a half hour and up for private lessons.

Incidentally, if you've never ridden before, it's probably a good idea to start your lessons in half-hour stretches. Your muscles will thank you (believe me!), and you'll progress faster because you'll be fresh each time you mount up.

Once you get established at a particular stable—that is, once you're more than just a face in the passing crowd—there are ways to get your own riding time free of charge. It's simple: you just change the medium of exchange. Instead of money you offer something you have (or can get) for something the stable needs.

Let me show you how this works. When I was in high school I persuaded my stable to let me ride an hour a week free in exchange for bringing in a regular group of paying customers. I formed a riding club of about six younger girls, brought them to the stable each week, and taught them myself. The experience I gained earned me a summer job later, as a camp riding counselor!

Other exchanges you might make for free riding time are stable work (so many hours cleaning out stalls for so much riding time), tack cleaning (same arrangement), or, if your're qualified, teaching beginners yourself. When you feel you know your instructor and the stable owner well enough, approach them. Most will be glad to have the extra help, and happy to help out someone who's really eager to learn. Just be sure you're capable of holding up your end of the bargain.

Going riding, of course, isn't all lessons and instructors. Nor is it all work—show preparation and the like. Riding is mostly fun. And that's what this book is about. Lots of people ride just because they love being outdoors, and because they love being with horses.

As soon as you've ridden enough to feel moderately comfortable on horseback, you should try taking to the trail. Not on an organized,

Riding students get a lesson from their instructor on how to show a horse at halter. The indoor riding arena is a feature of this teaching and boarding stable; classes and training can continue year-round, without interruptions by Old Man Weather.

fancy kind of trail ride, but just the simple kind where you head out the barn door alone or with a few friends, to take in the countryside.

A trail ride is a perfect day, a canter on flat ground, quiet contentment in the walking places. It's the thing to do when you want to think—or when you want to stop thinking at all for a while. Casual trail riding opens up a way of feeling about horses, about nature, and about yourself that nothing else can do in quite the same way.

My husband sings the praises of zipping through the woods on a motorcycle, and he's certainly not alone, judging from the noises coming out of those woods these days. But how can you hear the birds call and the leaves rustle when you've got hundreds of horsepower screaming under you? Give me the clop, clop of a single horse's hooves, please. The silent, steady sound of just one horsepower only adds to the peace I can find on the trail.

Trail riding is good for the way you feel about yourself. Both self-confidence and ability must go into handling a horse outside the riding ring; both are also necessary to the building of a healthy self. The combination of horse underneath and sky above, with nothing to fence you in, can be both a test and a thrill of the highest order.

Of course, warm and sunny weather just isn't around all the time. But a chill in the air is no reason to lock up the barn for the winter. If you learn to dress for the weather, you can ride in solid comfort all year round.

Long underwear and sweaters (layers of thin ones, not one big fat one) are the order of winter. To keep your toes from losing contact with your body, leave off your regular riding boots and instead wear layers of socks under slip-on winter boots. Mittens are warmer than gloves, of course, but if you ride with double reins you'll just have to take the consequences.

But the best warmer-upper of all is your horse! Just take the saddle off! Bareback riding in winter is the answer to barn-souring for both of you. So make it a point to learn how before the snow flies.

Riding for fun is really what it's all about. Once you've taken the trouble to learn the fundamentals of good horsemanship, the deepest satisfaction in riding comes from the one-to-one relationship you develop when it's just you and a horse together.

Where that relationship can lead depends on you both.

3

Project Horse

Once you've learned to ride a horse well enough to be pretty sure of staying on most of the time, what then? Why, find others to enjoy your fun with, of course!

Generally speaking, the best place to look for people who like horses is in the midst of a group of horse lovers. Younger or older, horse people are well organized into lots of different national clubs. Young horse people can pretty well pick and choose among several youth-oriented groups. Pick a specialty, choose a region, embrace a breed. Whatever your own personal interests are, you can be sure there's a national organization to serve you.

Youth horse groups come in as many sizes and shapes as the animal they love. Some, like the Pony Club, emphasize basic horsemanship and are oriented toward hunting and jumping. Groups like the big American Junior Quarter Horse Association draw their members from owners and fanciers of a particular breed of horses. Organizations like 4-H concern themselves with the agricultural end of the horse industry, while still others, the Scouts, are of a more general, community-oriented nature.

Should you join a horse group? And if so, which one suits you best? Let's look at some of the leading organizations and consider such things as purpose, activities, and memberships; then, perhaps, you can draw your own conclusions.

Perhaps the largest number of young horse people under one banner belong to the federally sponsored movement called 4-H. Nearly a quarter of a million kids from both rural and urban areas participate each year in 4-H Light Horse Projects. Combining horse management with horsemanship, the Project tries to meet a special need of today's young people.

The horse program usually involves 4-H members who own their own animals; it attempts to develop character, pride, and responsibility while teaching horsemanship, breeding, and training. 4-H graduates

A mounted Boy Scout troop takes to the woods to pursue their favorite sport. *Courtesy Boy Scouts of America.*

emerge from their Projects with a solid knowledge of safety and skill, too. They find themselves better prepared for life by their experiences with group work in community-sponsored horse projects and activities.

And they have a terrific amount of fun in the process. Their leaders, USDA Extension Specialists and adult volunteers, may conduct horsemanship clinics, field days, trail rides, horse shows—you name it and a 4-H Club has probably done it. Judging seminars and mounted drills and square-dance teams on horseback are other popular activities. Near you, there's already a 4-H Club in action.

4-H isn't strictly a horse-oriented group, of course—projects in beef, swine, and poultry also flourish, as do the Future Farmers of America, a national organization of vocational-agriculture students.

The Future Farmers, while focusing primarily on modern farming and ranching methods, also offer a "Horse Proficiency Award" as a special project of the National FFA Foundation and sponsored by the American Morgan Horse Foundation. Future Farmers compete among themselves in the categories of horse production and of horse-related supervised occupational experience. Applicants for the Award must keep careful monetary records, and supply the Foundation with statements of skills and achievements accumulated during the program. Horse Proficiency Awards are given on regional, state, and national levels.

Like 4-H and Future Farmers, Scouting is another area that is open to many, and that counts horse sports among its community-oriented activities.

Both the Boy Scouts of America and the Girl Scouts of the USA have special programs and badges that reflect the rapid growth of the horse's popularity with their members.

The Scout groups both sponsor mounted troops and patrols, and offer horse-related merit badges. The boys, for instance, may earn a Horsemanship badge when they've mastered the basic skills of riding and horse care. Cadet Girl Scouts (ages twelve to fourteen) have a similar Horsewoman badge that requires knowledge of basic riding skills and participation in an organized horse activity such as a show or trail ride. Younger girls can pursue an interest in horses by developing their own badge on the subject—the "Our Own Troop" badge. In fact, Girl Scout Headquarters lists the horse among the most popular of subjects for that badge.

In addition, both Scout groups offer specialized Western experience to older members. Girl Scouts go to Wyoming, and Boy Scouts to New Mexico.

According to Girl Scout Headquarters, "Saddle Straddle is a trail riding and conservation opportunity for 14- to 18-year-old girls, and is held annually at the Girl Scout National Center West in Ten Sleep, Wyoming. The event is open to 144 registered Girl Scouts. Two two-week sessions are offered for inexperienced riders, and two sessions for more experienced girls."

The focus of Saddle Straddle, says GS Headquarters, is on learning and reviving horsemanship skills. As part of the program, girls prepare for and take a six-day pack trip on unmarked trails of their own choosing, with only minimal adult supervision.

Philmont Boy Scout Ranch in Cimarron, New Mexico, offers a different sort of experience. Here boys move from one wilderness campsite to the next during their stay, and they encounter everything from bowhunting to gold mining to horseback riding along the way. The camp guide points to "a remuda of 250 horses," with "mountain horse rides at 8 A.M. and 1 P.M. daily."

Riding, grooming, exercising, showing, and just being around horses are popular activities with Scouts of all ages and both sexes. In communities where many own their own animals, riding becomes a natural extension of regular Scouting activities. In other places Scouts borrow or rent horses, take riding lessons together to perfect their skills, talk with veterinarians, and observe horses being fed, groomed, shod, and trained.

Reading, writing, and drawing about horses are popular too, and often crop up in other merit badges such as Books, Creative Writing, and Drawing and Painting. No doubt about it: horses and Scouts are a good match.

All of the organizations we've discussed so far probably are already in operation right where you are. But other, more specialized groups abound too, and though these may be a bit harder to find, their specialized programs certainly make it worth your while to either locate an ongoing program or start your own.

The United States Pony Clubs, Inc., or "Pony Club," is well known by most horse people for the quality of its instruction and for the quality of young riders who graduate from its programs. And the programs, despite their rather one-sided emphasis on hunting and jumping, are many sided.

Pony Clubs are designed to cover riding, horsemastership, and stable management for young people under twenty-one years of age. In 1975, forty-three states boasted 266 local clubs, with a total of over ten-thousand members. Pony Club offers programs in dressage, cross-country, stadium jumping, polo, tetrathalon, and gymkhana, to name a few. Meetings may be mounted or unmounted, and are called rallies. Unmounted meetings are classroom sessions in feeding, vetting, shoeing, judging, and the like.

Pony Clubbers are rated from "D" (the basics of horsemanship and stable management) through "A." The top "A" category not only requires the rider to be able to ride and train green horses over jumps; the Pony Club Handbook states that "An A Candidate should be able to explain what he is doing and why." Many an acclaimed horseman could never, ever, pass that "A" test.

A unique aspect of Pony Club is that older members help instruct the younger ones. In fact, both the A and B tests require knowledge and experience in the field of horsemanship instruction. The Pony Club publishes its own educational material, and maintains a film library for use by member clubs. Tests are conducted regularly in riding, hunting, and stable management; certificates of proficiency can be earned. In addition, Pony Club sponsors local, regional, and national rallies and awards.

Still another avenue of approach to the youth horse world is through the various breed organizations. For every breed club—and there are many—a youth group or section usually exists. Generally speaking, the aims and activities of these clubs are much like those of the general organizations we've already discussed. The major difference is this: all the members focus their interest on horses of the same breed, and on horse people who favor that breed.

To go through the aims and activities of each breed association would take forever and accomplish nothing. So let's focus for now on three of the largest groups' youth activities: the American Junior Quarter Horse Association (AJQHA), the Appaloosa Horse Club Youth Program, and the Junior Arabian Horse Club. You can get an idea of what all these groups do, and then get in touch with the association for the breed that interests you. (See Appendix II.)

Here, for example, is the statement of purpose for the junior Quarter Horse club: "The AJQHA is a division of the American Quarter Horse Association, for young men and women 18 years of age and under. It was organized primarily to improve and develop the skills of young people, both individually and through group participation, in the breeding, raising, and exhibition of American Quarter Horses."

Similarly, Arabian fanciers say, "The youth club provides a wholesome atmosphere where youth can make friends, where various activities will provide physical fitness, and where youth can relish the enjoyment of friends and of the Arabian horse."

The Appaloosa people are a little more specific. "Program objectives," they say, "are (1) to provide recognition for young people who currently own or show Appaloosas; (2) to stimulate interest in Appaloosa horses by participation in some phase of the Youth Program; (3) to promote a program with the ideals of citizenship, sportsmanship, showmanship, leadership, and to develop pride in owning an Appaloosa; and (4) to provide a variety of educational aids through which an understanding of the breed will be standardized throughout the United States."

Pretty lofty goals, no? But no matter how they say it, the objectives of all the breed clubs come out pretty much the same: education and encouragement of young horse people, and promotion of a particular breed of horse. All you need to start your own branch is enthusiasm and a few other local enthusiasts.

Opportunities and activities in the breed clubs are many. Movies, club newsletters and brochures, judging and horsemanship clinics, rule books, local and national award systems, youth shows and youth divisions of adult shows, even free or reduced stud services, colt leases,

These three girls exhibit some of the skills they've learned as members of a national horse-breed junior association. Whether they ride hunt style, Western style, or bareback, their form is as impeccable as the full-blooded horses they ride. *Courtesy Appaloosa Horse Club.*

and brood mare loans can be yours for the price of a membership—usually some paltry sum under five dollars a year. Some breed clubs even offer educational college scholarships to eligible members!

These national organizations are all well run. They know what they want, and they know how to get it for you.

But for sheer unadulterated fun, look around in your own backyard—and join a saddle club! These are the grass roots of all horse organizations. As a whole, they have more members than any other type of horse club. Saddle clubs are more disorganized and have more good times than just about anybody else.

No matter how many national organizations a horseman belongs to, he or she is almost sure to hold a membership in at least one local saddle club. In my area we have at least a dozen within a thirty-mile radius!

Just what is a saddle club? Well, activities and members are so varied that perhaps it's easiest to talk about what a saddle club is *not*.

For one thing, saddle clubs are almost unanimously independent. No national organization oversees or sponsors most local groups. So horse people are free to get together on their own, and organize their activities around whatever interests are strongest in their own membership areas. And they're free to make changes, too, as times and people change.

Also, saddle clubs don't generally limit their memberships by age, by interest, or by anything else. This does, of course, vary from area to area and from club to club. But generally speaking, saddle clubs are mostly just groups of people who love horses. Very often, you don't even have to own a horse to belong.

Sound like a good place to get to know the horses and horse people in your neck of the woods or stretch of the prairie? Well, it's one of the best.

So pick and choose. Local, national, international—they're all open to you. You can belong to just one group, like the Scouts; or two, like the Scouts and a saddle club; or —well, how many clubs can you fit into your schedule and still have time to visit Old Nellie occasionally?

The choices are yours. The opportunities are wide open.

4

How To Watch a Horse Show *

Imagine yourself in a ringside seat at the panorama of a horse show. It's summer, and floodlighting or hot sun or maybe even drizzle is streaming down. But nobody notices.

Feel the striding hoofbeats through your shoes. Listen to the loudspeaker and the music. Smell the mixture of hotdogs and horseflesh in the air. And feast your eyes on the shining animals parading round and round the show ring.

A horse show, any horse show, is a grand confusion of color and excitement. For anyone. But if you're a horse lover, a real horse nut, then horse shows can be something extra special to you while they add an extra dimension to your summer.

For horse shows are more than the excitement, the action, and the emotion. Much more. If you care enough, you can find out what's behind all that hullabaloo. And you'll end up with a new something-to-do in the horse world, and some valuable technical information, too.

In the show ring everything comes together for horse people. All the lessons, all the training, all the practice, all the careful grooming—here the reason finally shows up. Here everything finally makes sense.

Horse shows make sense. And not only to owners and riders. Anybody whose life revolves around the sound of hoofbeats and the feel of leather—you!—can be very much at home here.

Granted, at first glance a horse show has the appearance of a wild three-ring circus. Just the atmosphere is intoxicating. Why all those different classes? What are those people trying to do in that ring? What about all those *outside* the ring? Who's winning? And why?

If you've never been to a horse show before, your first visit will

*Adapted from "How to Watch a Horse Show" by Sally Stull from *Young Miss Magazine*, copyright © 1973 by Parents' Magazine Enterprises, Inc.

Horse show competitors come in all ages and sizes, and this little boy is no exception. Notice his calm and concentration—and his form—as he competes in a national breed horse show. *Courtesy Appaloosa Horse Club.*

probably throw you for a loop even if you think you know something about horses. So much is going on, and everyone who enters that ring has a different reason for being there.

"Rrrrrack on!" The announcer cries out, and sweat and foam fly as flashy Saddlebreds step out along the rail. Moments later, stocky Quarter Horses may weave surely through the intricacies of complex reining patterns.

Backyard pet ponies compete for trail horse trophies. And valuable purebreds strive right alongside them, toward the same goals.

Dusty cow horses race a clock and each other to a finish line. Then shining prancers strut their stuff under formal gear, for the discerning eye of the trained judge.

The whole affair is fascinating—but it can scramble your mind, too. Everyone seems to be operating under a set of strictly secret rules.

Understanding horse shows isn't really so secret, though. The key is in knowing how to watch, and knowing what to watch for. A little homework, a little close attention, a little understanding—and in no time you can be second-guessing those high-class judges. Really!

But before you can compete with the experts, you'd better master a few basics yourself. Some things you may know already; some may be news to you. All are important to learning about horse shows.

First and most basic of all is the distinction between the different ways people ride, and the ways their horses are trained. We discussed the terms "English" and "Western" riding in chapter 3. Well, in a horse show a Western class is one where the horse wears a Western (cowboy)

The Cloverleaf Barrel Race may be classed as a game event at some horse shows, but it's no game to this girl. The object is to get as close to the barrel as possible without knocking it—or your horse—down, and then racing against the clock after rounding three obstacles. *Courtesy Appaloosa Horse Club.*

saddle and the rider dresses casually. An English class calls for a "flat" saddle and more formal riding attire.

Another important point concerns the judging. After all, those ribbons and trophies are what everybody's in there for. Some classes are judged on the rider only, and not on the horse. Horsemanship, or equitation, is a good example; here the rider's style and control alone are under the judge's scrutiny. In other events the rider can almost be hanging by one stirrup and still win, provided the horse keeps his cool and does his job well. Pleasure and breed classes, performance classes and timed events are all strictly horse-oriented as far as judging is concerned.

There are other basic distinctions, too. Some classes limit riders, or horses, by age; rules may restrict entries by breed or residence as well.

This, after all is said and done, is what horse show competition is all about: the pride of accomplishment. But you can be sure this girl has had her share of days when there wasn't much accomplishment at all—just, perhaps, the knowledge of where she'd goofed and the resolve to try harder next time. *Courtesy Appaloosa Horse Club.*

By and large, this sort of stipulation is up to the horse show committee, and is made plain in the show program.

These, then, are the ground rules. They apply in one way or another to each of the many different classes that make up each horse show. But what actually makes the classes different? Why are there so many events? Who makes the rules? And how can the same horse and rider show—and win—in so many different classes?

Well, people own different kinds of horses, and they expect them to do different things. In the West, Quarter Horses and reining classes are apt to be most popular. In the East, it's Thoroughbreds and jumping (or Quarter Horses and jumping).

So horse show classes are set up mainly along the lines of breed and of performance, whether of the horse or of the rider. Rules for each class are, by and large, laid down by the American Horse Shows Association or some other governing body. Many horses, of course, can cross these artificial barriers and compete in all sorts of events. For some, the change is as simple as a switch of saddle from Western to English.

That rack the announcer asked for, now. In gaited classes the judge looks for a combination of collection, speed, and style. The girl out there in the blue riding habit may be smiling for all she's worth, but on the inside everything she's got is going toward turning out the best possible performance.

Gaited classes are the fanciest of all English events, and are by far the most formal in any show. Parade horse classes top the Western side for sheer showmanship. Then come the English and Western pleasure horse classes, and the just-for-fun games.

And for some competitors, that's just what a horse show is—a rip snortin' game. They weave at top speed through a row of tall poles, urge their mounts around a cloverleaf pattern of oil drums, and in general push themselves and their mounts to the physical limit. They enjoy the sport, their animals thrive, and horse show crowds shout themselves hoarse until the last tick of the stopwatch.

Sounds like fun, doesn't it? But faraway fun, perhaps—unless you know how to go about getting in on the action.

First, of course, you have to find the shows. Most local saddle clubs announce in the newspapers, and plaster the countryside with posters just to make sure. Or seek out your horse friends. Drop by your local stable or tack shop. They know, and they'll be glad to tell you.

Once you've arrived on the grounds, there are a couple of angles you can play to make the absolute most of your day. One is do-it-yourself judging, and the other is backstaging.

Do-it-yourself judging is educated second-guessing of the professionals. Watch the classes closely and choose your own ribbon winners. Then see how well your opinion agrees with the judge's. You can learn a lot from this game, incidentally, if you're willing to notice the differences and to check back to see where you might have been wrong.

Backstage among the horse trailers is where you'll experience firsthand the preparation and anticipation that precede each animal into the ring. It's easiest to get into this area if you have a friend who's showing, but even strangers can stroll the back lot at most small horse shows. Just don't get in anyone's way! Some people may be glad to talk to you when they have a minute, but approaching them when they're saddling up to get into the ring is definitely not the right minute. A horse show is a busy place, after all. And that, of course, is half its charm.

Local horse shows may be exciting, but just look what happens when you attend one of international reputation. Here a rider at the Dublin (Ireland) Horse Show has lost all points of contact with his horse except for the reins. Think he made it? *Courtesy Irish Tourist Board.*

The rest is left to the horses themselves, and to the horse people. You can see the best animals in your area at a local horse show, and the best animals in the country at a national show.

The biggest of the Really Big Shows is held each fall in Madison Square Garden in New York City. Maybe you've seen it on television—maybe you've even been lucky enough to attend. Many of the classes here are a sort of finals competition, as riders who've accumulated points in their areas compete against one another.

But you don't need to go to Madison Square Garden to see a great horse show. There's probably one in your own backyard, this weekend. So go find yourself a horse show. Get out in the sun and cheer for your favorites. Learn a little more about the horse world. And have some fun!

Really, now. Shouldn't there be horse shows in your summer?

5
Rodeo!

Horse shows may have splendor all sewed up, but for pure unadulterated thrills, nothing in the horse world tops a rodeo.

Here as nowhere else the thunder of hooves, the clouds of dust, the roars of the crowd are the stuff of which excitement is made. Here man struggles against man, against beast, and with horse against beast. And for what? Why, for the sheer glory of doing the same thing all over again next week at the very next rodeo up the pike!

Although the American West is still rodeo's main stamping ground, today's professional cowboy is nearly as likely to hail from New Jersey as from Montana—and may even be female!

You might say that rodeo cowboys are both born *and* made. Rodeo clubs abound for young riders, with organized competition beginning at age eight for both boys and girls. Western high schools and colleges compete fiercely in intramural rodeo; emotions run as high as at any Eastern football game.

Why all the whoop-de-doo and hi-yi-yipee? Well, let's visit a junior rodeo and find out!

Once inside the grounds, your senses will be overwhelmed. Listen to the bawling of cattle, the whinny of horses, the arena bullhorns, the crowd—they're all there. And the smells are, too—horses, hotdogs, and cows! Are you in the mood?

Okay. Events at a junior rodeo vary according to the sponsoring organization. But usually they boil down into three general categories: riding, roping, and roughhousing.

All rodeo events are timed, in the sense that each contestant enters the ring alone and races against the clock. The person to complete the action in the shortest time, and by the rules, wins the event.

In riding competitions you have mad dashes the length of the arena to pick up and drop off flags. Cloverleaf barrel racing and pole bending

Calf-roping is perhaps the best-known—and most controversial—event in rodeo. This young rider has lassoed his calf, and already the horse is sliding to a stop that will jerk the calf off his feet. Then the rider must dismount and tie three of the calf's legs securely; best time wins. Humanitarians object to the force with which 250 pounds of calf reaches the end of the taut rope. *Photo by James Fain, courtesy National High School Rodeo Assn.*

both involve rushing around obstacles in intricate patterns.

Occasionally two classes are included in rodeo that fit equally well into horse shows: trail horse and cutting horse. Trail horses are required to complete a varied obstacle course, and cutting horses must contend with live obstacles—cattle. The rider and horse must separate as many as possible from the herd within a given time limit.

Roping events go under many different names, and use different animals and different methods. But a roper usually needs just about equal parts of personal skill, horse help, and pure dumb luck to win with any regularity.

Calf roping is probably the event most familiar to most people. It's sometimes called Catch as Catch Can, which is well put. You've seen this one on television. Horse, rider, and calf come charging down the arena together at full speed, the calf only a few jumps ahead of the horse. The object is to rope the calf, throw him to the ground (some of them weigh as much as 350 pounds!), and tie any three legs together—quickly. The rider who can accomplish this in the shortest time wins the event, though I'm sure many a junior rodeoer is quite pleased to accomplish it at all. In a similar event called Breakaway Roping, contestants are required to rope the calf but not to tie it.

Other roping events require partnership not only between horse and rider, but between two riders. Double Mugging is essentially calf roping with an on-the-ground helper who assists in downing the calf. In Team Tying both mounted riders must rope the calf "head and heel"; Dally Team Roping is another version of the same song. Ribbon Roping requires a rider to rope the calf and with a helper remove a ribbon from its tail, running with the ribbon to the finish line for timing.

Then you have the roughhouse events, the ones people gladly broil in the hot sun or soak in driving rain to see. Here, folks, we have steer wrestling, steer and bull riding, and saddle and bareback bronc riding. Each is exactly what the name says. And each is backed with enough thrills to last rider and spectator both for a long time—or at least until the next rodeo.

Also included in roughhouse events is Goat Tying—usually a class for girls and junior boys. A goat is tethered at the far end of the arena. On signal the rider races toward the animal, dismounts, throws it to the ground, and ties three feet together. Again, fastest time wins.

Does this sound like your cup of mud? If it does, you'd do well to get in touch with one of the many associations sponsoring juvenile rodeo. Four groups seem to cover much of the territory; which one suits you best depends in part on how old you are, and in part on what group is active in your area. The Little Britches and American Junior

Bronc riders don't always look this graceful when they part company with their steeds. This one may not have felt too graceful, either. *Photo by Gustafson Rodeo Photography, courtesy National High School Rodeo Assn.*

rodeo associations cater to kids from about eight to twenty. The High School and Intercollegiate associations have chapters in various schools. If you're a Westerner, you're in luck. If you live in the East and have rodeo dust in your blood, though, the action will be a lot tougher to find.

Let's look at the general organizations first. The National Little Britches Rodeo Association (2160 South Holly, Suite 105, Denver, Colorado 80222) is a franchise "open to all nonprofit organizations interested in furthering the objectives and aims of the association, and extending the influence of better junior rodeo." Although press releases claim members "from the West Coast to the East Coast and from Canada to Mexico," most sanctioned Little Britches events take place west of the Mississippi.

This is goat-tying, an event for girls and junior boys that isn't quite as rough as calf-roping, but has its thrills and skills nonetheless. *Photo by Gustafson Rodeo Photography, courtesy National High School Rodeo Assn.*

Little Britches contestants compete in two age groups: juniors (ages eight to thirteen) and seniors (fourteen to seventeen). Anyone in these age groups who isn't a member or permit holder in a collegiate or adult rodeo association is eligible to join Little Britches. The annual membership fee includes both medical and life insurance plus rule book, lapel pin, membership card, arm patch, and a subscription to the *National Little Britches Rodeo News.*

Membership in the American Junior Rodeo Association (103 West College, Sonora, Texas 76950) is open to anyone who's under nineteen and unmarried. Members are not limited to within the bounds of the continental United States but come from Canada and Mexico as well. This association attempts to "organize junior cowboy and cowgirl rodeos of the United States, Canada, and Mexico." In addition, Junior

Steer-riding is probably the most dangerous sport in juvenile rodeo. Judging from the gleem in this bull's eye and the air space between it and the rider, the animal may well have won this round. *Photo by Gustafson Rodeo Photography, courtesy National High School Rodeo Assn.*

association members are encouraged to "promote scholastic attainment and discourage sacrificing school attendance and grades to participate in rodeos during the school year." Competitors are divided into three age groups: twelve and under, thirteen to fifteen, and sixteen to seventeen.

The National High School Rodeo Association (Box 95, Edgar, Montana 59026) got its start when a superintendent of schools helped sponsor a small local rodeo. Noting the interest he and his students shared, he came up with the idea of trying out rodeo as a high school sport. The idea took. Now the association has both state and national finals competition, and member schools in most Western states.

The National Intercollegiate Rodeo Association (P.O. Box 2088, Huntsville, Texas 77340) claims more than two hundred colleges and over twenty-five-hundred students as members. Unlike most of the other youth rodeo groups, Intercollegiate has an "Ozark" region that

Bull-dogging, team roping, double-mugging—what ever you call this event, the calf seems destined to get the worst of it. *Photo by James Fain, Courtesy National High School Rodeo Assn.*

Barry Burk, a veteran timed-event contestant from Duncan, Oklahoma, is in good shape getting down on this steer in the exciting event of steer wrestling. Now Burk has to bring the animal to a stop, and by applying leverage to his horns, throw him to the ground. Time is stopped by the "flagger" when the steer is on his side, with head and hooves pointed in the same direction. Times of four seconds or less are not uncommon in this event. *Photo by Ferrell Butler, courtesy Rodeo Cowboys Assn.*

includes states *east* of the Mississippi. Rodeo buffs in Alabama, Mississippi, and Tennessee can root for their own schools at the Intercollegiate National Finals Rodeo, often featured on network television.

According to the Intercollegiate association, "College rodeo clubs are officially recognized on their respective campuses. They provide, in addition to representing their institutions in rodeo competition opportunities for social and service outlets to the college community." Many rodeo clubs sponsor Western Weeks, trail rides, barbecues, and square dances along with other activities which they feel help to preserve Western tradition and sentiment.

Member schools may be junior colleges, four-year colleges, or universities. All schools must be nationally accredited; each rodeo club must have at least six members to start. "However," the group adds, "individuals are invited to represent their institutions and compete regionally and nationally on an individual basis."

After college many youth members go on to join one of the professional rodeo organizations. Best known of these is the Rodeo Cowboys Association, called the RCA (2929 West 19th Ave., Denver, Colorado 80204). RCA-sanctioned rodeos don't stay at home on the range, though of course they're more numerous there. RCA rodeos are held annually in such unlikely states as Vermont, Virginia, and Florida. More than forty states and four Canadian provinces now hold over six hundred RCA events every year, and there's no slow-down of interest in sight.

According to the RCA, more than three thousand cowboys hold professional memberships, and more than ten million people a year pay to see them perform. RCA rodeos offer more than five million dollars in prize money each year—ample incentive to hit the dirt just one more time.

All the youth rodeo groups welcome girls into their membership, and any girl who wants to "turn pro" has access to a professional organization, the Girls Rodeo Association, or GRA (8909 N.E. 25th St., Spencer, Oklahoma 73084). Although there's no lower age limit, child labor laws in some states require members under twenty-one to supply written approval of parent or guardian. But this is no female protection agency. GRA members ride bareback broncs, bulls, and steers. They round the barrels at breakneck speed; they rope and tie calves; they even "undecorate steers"—that is, they pull off a ten-inch ribbon taped to the back of a charging hulk of beef. The GRA has Eastern, Southern, and Central regions along with Western regions, and works cooperatively with the Canadian Girls' Rodeo Association.

Another large professional rodeo organization is the International Rodeo Association, or IRA (P.O. Box 615, Pauls Valley, Oklahoma 73075). This group has the same general aims and functions as the RCA, although a semifriendly rivalry is maintained. (In 1972 the IRA issued a challenge to the RCA that the champions in each organization meet for a World Series Rodeo. The event has yet to come about.) In addition, the IRA recognizes barrel racing as a championship event, while the RCA does not. In 1973, two girls were among the top ten money-winners in the IRA.

Historically, rodeo riders came straight in off the range and spent their days off from running cattle and busting broncs by busting cattle and giving the broncs a run for the money. Today, obviously, things have changed. Rodeo is taught in the public schools, and girls hold their own with men.

Girls aren't limited anymore to rodeo competitions like barrel-racing, pole-bending, and goat-tying. They have their own professional association and rodeos, which feature such events as bareback bronc riding and the dangers of Brahma bull riding. *Courtesy Girls Rodeo Assn.*

Girls rodeo competition.

Today would-be cowboys can come from anywhere in the country. Big city cowboys don't fall any harder than the ranch boys, and the money's the same for both. The main difference is experience and exposure. And the rodeo world has come up with a way to shorten that gap as well: the rodeo riding school.

These rodeo seminars are run on a commercial basis by such top rodeo greats as Jim Shoulders (Henryetta, Oklahoma) and Larry Mahan (Mesquite, Texas). They're week-long intensive training courses in rodeo skills. Here, if you're interested, you can learn saddle bronc, bareback bronc, or bull riding. You pay by the event; fees include room and board and "all the stock you want." Some schools even feature a mechanical bucking bronco that's reputed to be capable of just as many dirty tricks as the real live ones. Dates for the schools are advertised regularly in Western horse publications.

Rodeo, then, has come a long ways from the days of little infights

Rodeo clowns need more skill, more guts, and more pure dumb luck than anyone else in the rodeo game. Their job is to attract the vicious Brahma bulls away from fallen riders; they can get into a lot of trouble in the process. Fortunately, this clown wasn't hurt, but it's still a risky business. *Courtesy International Rodeo Assn.*

between rival trail herd crews. Today thousands of people live and breathe rodeo; hundreds depend on it in some form for their total livelihood.

Is there a place for you among the thrills of rodeo? Well, look around and see!

Nobody ever said rodeo wasn't a dirty business. *Courtesy National High School Rodeo Assn.*

6

The Hunt *

Imagine a crisp fall day in the country—a calendar pin-up sort of day. The open fields have rock and rail fences, and fall color has just passed its peak. Add a dash of briskness to the air. Now paint in horses of all colors, and brown-white-black hounds, and riders in bright scarlet coats. And somewhere in the underbrush, don't forget to hide Old Brer Fox.

There now. You have all the basic elements for one of the horse world's most exciting and most demanding sports—fox hunting!

Want to paint yourself into that picture? Well, depending on where you live and who you know, that can be as easy as falling off a horse (which happens quite often in the hunt field) or almost impossible.

The main requirement is that you live in, or at least near, what's called "hunt country." This means two things: first, that the landowners have agreed to allow limited hunting on horseback over their fields; and second, that an organized Hunt Club sees to it that fox hunts are conducted in an orderly fashion, and that any damage to the land is promptly rectified. Hunts exist in almost every state; if you're not sure whether there's one near you, check the annual foxhunting issue of the magazine *The Chronicle of the Horse,* which is published in Middleburg, Virginia.

The next obstacle to be hurdled is more political than physical: securing the right to ride with a particular hunt. For juniors, this isn't so easy. Anybody can enter a horse show or a rodeo—all you need is the price of the entry fee. Hunts, however, are a lot fussier. And they have their reasons.

*Portions of an excellent pamphlet on hunting, *Riding to Hounds in America,* are quoted with the permission of the author, William P. Wadsworth, and of the publisher, Alexander Mackay-Smith of *The Chronicle of the Horse.*

This photo gives a good illustration of the hunt field. In front is the Whipper-In (assistant to the Huntsman); at right is the Huntsman (in charge of the hounds); in the center foreground is the Master of Foxhounds, or MFH, head of the whole shebang. In the background is the field, led by a Field Master. *Photo by Harriet Hatchell, courtesy Huntlea Horse Center.*

Let's look at the ways in which young people can hunt. You may be a member of a hunting family that pays membership dues of several hundred dollars a year for the privilege. You may tag along with a hunt member as a guest, in which case your riding ability must be vouched for by that member, and you must be approved by the leader of the hunt, called the Master of Fox Hounds, or MFH. Guest privileges are usually limited to a certain number of hunts—say three—per season. Or you may belong to a junior horse group like Pony Club that sponsors its own hunts or is invited to hunt with the local adult group.

You cannot invite yourself to a hunt. You must know somebody who's a member, and they must know you well enough to be sure of your riding skills. If not, then you're out until you're eighteen and old enough (and rich enough) to buy your own membership.

The only time regulations are relaxed is during the preseason "cub-hunting." This takes place in early fall, and is a rather informal affair designed primarily to introduce young hounds, green horses, and inexperienced riders to the sport. If at all possible, you should go cubbing long before you ever put in an appearance with the formal hunt.

Many hunts allow young people to cub-hunt as often as they please, and don't count cub hunts as regular "guest" invitations. Still, be sure you know the policy of the hunt you'll be with—don't just show up at even a cub meet and expect to be welcomed with open arms. Check with the Secretary or the MFH first; make sure your presence will be acceptable.

Sounds stuffy, right? Well, from a young person's point of view it probably is. But let's take a look at the Hunt Club's side of things.

What would happen to a hunt if anyone who wanted to could ride along? Mayhem would be the result, and here's why.

Hunts charge fairly large membership fees to cover the many costs of maintaining their hounds and their country. The fees also serve another

Here's everybody's dream hunt country—beneath an ancient castle in County Tipperary, Ireland. The Huntsman (center) and his two Whippers-in see to the hounds as they check out the scent of the vanished fox. *Courtesy Irish Tourist Board.*

purpose: the size of the hunting field (those who come along for the ride) can be regulated. And this is absolutely necessary. Because a hunt is responsible for the territory it covers, the field of riders must be small enough to control. A hundred riders tend to zap off in all directions, fifty or less can be watched by a member of the hunt staff appointed to do just that—the Field Master.

Another reason hunts limit their memberships is the degree of horsemanship skill necessary to make hunting safe for all concerned. Fences in the field may begin at three feet six inches, which in itself requires a fair amount of skill to negotiate. But just because you can do it in the lesson ring doesn't mean you can manage a big jump in the midst of a bunch of clamoring hunters raring to go. Every time a horse or rider goes down, the rest of the Hunt must wait while that person or animal removes himself from the scene—or is removed, depending on the severity of the fall. And every time a horse refuses, the field of riders behind packs up even more, and may even cause the refuser to get scrunched up against the fence.

After all, this is a *hunt,* not a leisurely cross-country trail ride with a few jumps thrown in for fun. When the hounds are on a line, the riders want to be right behind the hounds. Anyone who gets in their way will be extremely unpopular—and may be accidentally injured, to boot.

Then, too, hunts have the ever-present problem of leaving the farmers' lands in as good a condition as before they were hunted over. This means closing gates, reporting and repairing damage, and not stumbling through someone's newly planted field. Inexperienced hunters are very likely to be ignorant of such rules, and unable anyway to cope with them.

So hunts do limit their memberships. And although their reasons are sound, they do tend to keep a number of young horsemen at bay.

But suppose you *do* know somebody who invites you to hunt. Or suppose you check with the Hunt Secretary and get a favorable response to your questions about new members and guests. Or suppose your youth horse club is ready to try its skill in the hunt field. Then what? What should you know in advance? And what can you expect to happen?

To begin with, you can read all you want on hunting before you go, and you should do just that. (An excellent pamphlet on the subject is *Riding to Hounds in America* by William P. Wadsworth, MFH.)

But you can expect to be a total novice in spite of all your book-learning, and you should take absolutely no action on your own once you're in the hunt field. Don't lead anyone, don't make any unnecessary noises, watch out for the hounds, and do your best to stay toward the rear of the field. And be positive you can handle your horse.

As Mr. Wadsworth cautions in his pamphlet, "Remember that the most important gait in a hunter is the halt. If your horse won't stand, teach him. If he won't learn, sell him. If he won't sell, shoot him." Sound advice, for the cardinal sin in the hunt field is for a rider to pass up or interfere in any way with one of the hunt staff.

The most important piece of clothing for hunting is the hard hat, and here again Mr. Wadsworth lays out a few guidelines.

"If you have passed early childhood," he says, "never wear a hunting cap without being sure that the MFH approves. The cap is a symbol of authority, to be worn only by the staff and other persons singled out by the MFH. The cap has the advantage that it is better protection against superficial scalp wounds, and does not cause the wind to interfere with your hearing. A well-made, well-fitting, reinforced hunting bowler or top hat is far better protection against more serious injury. Furthermore, it keeps the rain from going down your neck far better than a cap, and it protects your cheeks and ears while going through light brush."

So if you've been jumping at home in a regular hunt cap, you may be in need of some new equipment. But as with anything you may buy new for hunting, be sure you check with a hunting friend first. Hunting and all that surrounds it is strictly traditional, and the old hands you'll be hunting with take a rather dim view of young upstarts who get their signals all crossed up before they even get to the meet.

Which brings us to the problem of arriving at the appointed place. If you can't ride there, you'll have to depend on wheeled transportation, and Mr. Wadsworth points out with more than a grain of truth that "a vehicle cared for by a horseman is rather apt to be in the same condition as a horse cared for by a mechanic." So check out your transportation thoroughly the day before the meet.

Then get there well before the announced time. The MFH and the Huntsman (the staff member in charge of the hounds) may allow a few minutes for what Mr. Wadsworth calls "a difference in watches—no one ever admits that anyone *could* be late at a meet." But they won't wait for you.

The Huntsman with his hounds—never call them dogs!—and his Whippers-In (helpers) get the show on the road with his own personal language of voice and horn signals. But the person you watch is the Field Master, the one in charge of all the riders except the staff. The Field Master has a dual responsibility: to keep the riders out of the way of hounds, and to assure everybody a good, sporting hunt. Watch his actions, and pace your own accordingly.

A word here about the "sport" of hunting itself. There are, of course, more practical methods of eliminating a few foxes from a territory than to have fifty people on fifty horses chasing pell-mell after twenty-five couples of hounds who are following one small if crafty little animal. Mr. Wadsworth says admiringly of the fox, "I am convinced that he also is a sportsman and has a sense of humor, as I can see no other reason for a fox to stay above ground and permit himself to be hunted in a country so full of convenient holes as his own."

Mr. Wadsworth admits, "It is frankly (although not frequently) admitted that the method herein described is *not* an economically efficient method of killing foxes. If that was our purpose we could do it much more cheaply by use of poison and traps, but it is not. We hunt foxes with hounds and follow hounds on horseback because it is fun, and a good, healthy sport."

There are, of course, many humane society people who are in sharp disagreement with the foxhunters over their methods and means. They claim the hunters practice extreme cruelty by running a small animal in terror for miles and miles, only to have him pounced upon and torn to shreds by eager hounds at the journey's end.

Hunts often find themselves picketed by such groups, and may even admit that they do have a point. Indeed, most hunts today don't end with a kill at all, but rather with the fox "going to ground," or retreating to one of his underground burrows.

Many hunts also rely on "drag hunts," either for humane reasons or because their areas have simply run out of foxes. A drag hunt is one where the scent is laid previously by a Hunt staffer. It's up to the hounds to follow it through, and to the staffer to provide a good trail. Another form of foxless hunting is the "paper chase," where the emphasis is on riding, not hounds, as the staff leads the field in search of a number of previously scattered bits of paper.

In any case, riders may spend hours in the hunt field casting, running, sitting, and casting again until the fox—or whatever—is finally accounted for in one way or another. Then the hounds are congratulated, and the field dismissed.

Riding back slowly with the excitement of the chase still lingering is a most pleasant way to end a day.

7
Trail Rides and Riders

Trail riding is one of the oldest of all riding activities. Riders explored new lands on horseback and opened new trails. Settlers followed those trails toward their dreams; soldiers policed old trails and laid down new ones in their efforts to fulfill their duties.

Today trail riding has almost as many branches as the old trail West, and almost as many devotees. Some riders specialize in long-distance treks over rough terrain; they call it endurance, or competitive, riding. Others are deeply concerned with the preservation of old riding trails and the development of new ones; these are the pleasure riders.

Let's look at the distance folk first. An annual long ride may be sponsored by a saddle club—it may even achieve national recognition, as has the 100-Mile Competitive Trail Ride of the Green Mountain Horse Association in South Woodstock, Vermont. Rides like this attract people from all over the country, and are judged on speed and time (riders are penalized for finishing too quickly and too slowly), on physical condition of the horse, on horsemanship (both on and off the ground), and on proper navigation of a marked course.

Competitive trail rides probably started out as races to see who could get from one place to another in the shortest time with a live horse still under him. But times have changed. Competent, licensed veterinarians check the animals' condition frequently, before, during, and after the ride. Championships can be lost by the person who pushes his horse too hard in the name of speed, and by the rider who lags his animal in order to protect his physical condition.

One organization whose prime concern is the sanctioning of competitive trail rides under a uniform judging system is the North American Trail Ride Conference (NATRC). According to the group's president, the main objective of competitive riding is "to work all of

This fourteen-year-old girl has been riding "all her life," and entered her first competitive trail ride when she was nine. Here Sandi, dressed for the weather, concentrates on saving her horse and making time, both together. *Courtesy the North American Trail Ride Conference.*

the horses over an identical trail in the same length of time, thereby having a basis of fair comparison for determining the horse's soundness, condition, and manners. While this is not a race, judgment in timing and pacing is important; the winner usually is the one who rode his horse at a consistent pace throughout the ride, rather than 'hurrying up and waiting.'

"Competitive trail riding," says NATRC, "is the one form of horse activity that does not require expensive tack, riding lessons, or a registered, trained horse. All that is required is a fit horse and rider."

Interested? Well, let's look in on a typical two-day NATRC ride, as described by NATRC officials.

"The competitors begin arriving early Friday afternoon at the site selected as Ride Headquarters. After setting up camp (rules require all horses to be stabled under uniform conditions, tied to trees, trailers, fences, etc.) the horses are presented to the judges for a very thorough physical exam. Any scars, blemishes, or unsoundnesses are noted on the judging card. Following dinner, maps of the trail are distributed and discussed, and the judges conduct an informal question and answer period.

"On Saturday morning the horses are led to the start. The riders are timed out at 30-second intervals after mounting in front of the judges, who watch critically for both horsemanship and manner on the part of the horse.

"After leaving the start, the riders may travel at their own pace during the day, following trails marked with colored ribbons tied to trees or lime-white markers on the ground, as well as the map which shows turns, elevations, and mileage reference points along the route. The horses are observed several times during the day, often at a surprise point at the top of a steep climb where the pulse and respiration counts of each horse are taken by a team of veterinary assistants. The results of these 'P and R' checks are used by the judges as an aid in determining the overall condition of the horses.

"After a mandatory one-hour lunch and rest stop, the riders continue along the route to a point two miles from the finish. While the riders have been able to stop anywhere they choose up to this point, the rules require that forward motion be maintained during the last two miles, thereby insuring that all horses arrive at the finish in approximately the same state of physical exertion.

"After the finish on Saturday, the riders have until 10 P.M. to care for their mounts; no handling whatsoever is permitted thereafter until the Sunday morning judges' examination. The horses are carefully watched during the night by the stable steward; any horses appearing abnormal are brought to the immediate attention of the ride veterinarian and the owner.

"After the morning examination, during which the horses are trotted in hand to show any adverse effects of the previous day's ride, the horses are saddled and prepared for the final day's ride, which is conducted in the same manner as the first but over different trails.

"The weekend ends with an awards dinner early Sunday evening."

Most NATRC rides are held in the West, but as interest in competitive riding grows sanctioned events are beginning to move East. For more information about locations and membership write NATRC, 1995 Day Road, Gilroy, California 95020.

"Competitive riding," NATRC cautions, "should not be confused with endurance riding. The latter sport, also gaining in popularity, is

Moving up a steep grade, eleven-year-old Steve gets well out of his saddle to take weight off the horse's hindquarters. Steve, Sandi's sister, and his family all hold memberships in a competitive trail ride organization. *Courtesy North American Trail Ride Conference.*

Moving up a steep grade.

actually a controlled race against time over a given distance of generally 50 to 100 miles."

If this sort of long-distance horse racing sounds like fun, then you should check out the American Endurance Ride Conference (P.O. Box 1605, Auburn, California 95603). According to this organization, "The term *endurance riding* is defined as an athletic event in which the same horse and rider cover a measured course (usually 50 to 100 miles) and conforms to the following conditions:

"1. The first horse to finish in the least amount of time and in acceptable condition is the winner.

2. There shall be an award for the best conditioned horse.

3. There can be no minimum time limit.

4. The ride must be controlled by veterinarians.

5. Everyone finishing the ride shall receive a completion award.

6. The ride is open to all breeds of horses."

So while competitive and endurance riding may overlap in some areas, the prime distinction between the two seems to be fairly clear. Competitive riders place more emphasis on the all-around performances of their animals, while endurance riders tend to emphasize speed.

Basic procedure for an endurance ride is much the same as for a competitive ride, with a few notable exceptions. Endurance riders leave the base camp in a group, and are turned loose a couple of miles down the trail to fend for themselves. According to the AERC, "Some riders will take off on the dead run, some at a slower gallop, some at a fast trot, and some at a slow trot. If this is your first ride," they advise, "COOL IT!"

The AERC also offers a few other suggestions to beginning endurance riders. "When you come upon a group of horses that you are going to pass, don't just zoom through them." Conference officials suggest that you "Ask for the trail, but only where it is safe to pass. Don't push past anyone and endanger them if the trail is narrow. Hold back until you can safely get by.

"Another don't," the AERC continues, "is tailgating. Maybe your horse doesn't mind being followed closely, but many do. So give them room.

"Getting lost is another little goodie that does happen," the AERC admits. And advises, "Don't blame the rest of the world because you're all alone in the boondocks. Retrace your steps until you find a marker, check out horse tracks in the dirt, look for another marker, and go from there.

"The possibility of breaking equipment is always a factor, too. Swear, carry extra leather thongs, use your belt, tie knots, walk, and just realize that's a part of the sport."

Somehow, after all these trials and tribulations, you should manage to reach the finish line. "Smile!" the AERC commands. "Kiss your horse on the nose, and hug your helpers. See to your horse and then—go soak your bod in a nice hot tub!"

Both competitive and endurance ride groups claim a large number of junior members and offer separate point systems for them, along with reduced membership dues. Rides are scored on an individual basis, and points are accumulated toward regional and national titles in various categories.

As with competitive rides, endurance riding is mainly concentrated in the West. But their popularity is spreading too, and rides often take place as far East as Alabama and the Carolinas.

The third form of trail riding is probably the one most riders turn to first: just plain pleasure rides. This sort of thing used to be just as easy as heading out the barn door and across the fields. For some, it still is. But with today's increasing urbanization and automobilization, pleasure trails are getting harder and harder to find.

Enter the National Trails Council (53 W. Jackson Blvd., Chicago, Illinois 60604), which has set itself up as "a national body organized to support the planning, promotion, and execution of trails systems at the local, county, state, regional, and national levels; to establish guidelines for all kinds of trails; and to effect land use planning."

This group, then, is not involved strictly with horse people, but with all kinds of people, animals, and machines wishing to visit the American countryside.

"The National Trails Council," says its bulletin, "representing as it does people interested in trails for hikers, snowmobilers, bicyclists, canoeists, motorcyclists, skiers, equestrians, the handicapped, naturalists, etc., recognizes that difficulties may arise in many areas." How compatible, for instance, are a horse and a motorcycle on the same trail? And yet, how would the competitive and endurance rides operate if their crew couldn't be moved from place to place by jeep? Everybody's got to get together.

And they have, because for all these different types of people with their different kinds of sports, the trails are vital to all. "Common concern," says the Council, "has already paved the way for cooperation to find methods of compromise, and for providing trails for all with a minimum of conflict." For a group just begun in 1971, much as already been accomplished.

So if riding round and round in a ring just isn't your style, then consider trail riding in one of its many forms. Are you a perfectionist? Try competitive riding. Do you like the whistle of wind in your ears? Join an endurance ride. Or if you're just plain lazy and like the quiet of the woods, take a pleasure ride.

Tomorrow.

8

Are You Olympic Material?

The one horse activity that captures the hearts and minds of the whole world is the Olympic Equestrian Games. Held every four years, this competition features the absolute cream of the equine and equestrian crop in difficult and involved tests of training, endurance, and skill.

If you've watched the Olympics on television, you know how you can almost feel the tension crackling across the air waves. Only the best compete here, and national honor is at stake.

But how is the U.S. Equestrian Team chosen? Who, finally, competes in international games? And what sort of training would you need if someday you wanted to be a member of that team?

Well, let's take a look at its supporting organization first. The United States Equestrian Team, or USET (located at Gladstone, New Jersey 07934), is made up of competitors, trainers, and just plain interested folks who "undertake to advance international good will and promote better understanding of the United States through the medium of international equestrian sport."

Supported wholly by contributions to its cause, the USET "accepts full responsibility for training, equipping, and financing riding teams of the highest standard possible, to represent the United States in the Pan-American and Olympic Games, and in other international competitions."

This, obviously, is a big bite to chew. But the performance of our team has more than warranted the effort behind it. At home, for instance, USET riders have won over 250 international competitions, and the United States team has led the overall team standings in ten of the last twelve years. Our Three-Day Team is presently world champion in international standings; the Dressage Team is fifth.

But what do these terms mean, anyway? What is a Three-Day Event? Dressage? What's that? Just what's involved in Olympic Games competition?

The USET explains it this way. "Games programs," officials say, "call for three different contests, each performed by a different, specially trained squad.

"Dressage is a very searching test of the horse's obedience and responsiveness in performing prescribed classical movements on the flat.

"Prize of Nations is the most demanding form of stadium, or show-ring, jumping, requiring teams of three or four riders to twice negotiate a course of 16 to 20 artificial fences ranging up to 5 feet 3 inches in height and 7 feet 3 inches in breadth.

"The Three-Day Event is a test of versatility, which demands that the same horse and rider perform elementary dressage on the first day of competition; a twenty-mile speed and endurance phase (including steeplechase and cross-country jumping courses) on the second; and stadium jumping on the third."

Just reading the requirements makes you want to pause to catch your breath. The skill and dedication demanded of these riders and their horses places them far out of the league of most horsemen's wildest dreams.

But say your dream does include competition on the USET, someday. Where do you start? What must you learn? And what will be required of you?

Bill Steinkraus, president of the USET and Olympics gold-medal winner, has this advice for you.

"There's really nothing very complicated about the question which

Bill Steinkraus and Main Spring.

Bruce Davidson and Plain Sailing.

heads this chapter," Mr. Steinkraus says. "You're Olympic material if you're one of the three or four best riders in the country in one of the three Olympic equestrian disciplines.

"The question of whether or not you have Olympic potential is a bit more complicated, for Olympic potential is not all that rare. There are probably thousands of young riders who have sufficient talent as such, but who lack the drive or self-discipline to develop it to the Olympic level, or are unwilling to make the sacrifices it entails.

"The only way to find out if you have the potential," Mr. Steinkraus continues, "is to develop your talent, technique, and experience as far as you can, moving up the competitive ladder until you can cope with the demands made at the highest levels. There are," he warns, "no shortcuts."

It seems, then, that if you're shooting for a berth on the USET, then you're going to have to do a lot of eat-sleep-work horses before you make the grade.

"I think," Mr. Steinkraus adds, "that kids benefit from the attempt to see how far they can develop their talents. But," he cautions, "it is unfair to them to minimize how high the standard is at the top. Olympic riders are usually totally dedicated, and few kids are willing to make that kind of commitment. As a practical matter, kids who are waiting to be told that they're Olympic material probably aren't, because if they were, they would already be competing successfully on the highest levels."

Sobering thought. After all, only about fifteen riders make the Olympic Team. Out of how many thousand hopefuls?

But if you're still holding tight to your Olympic dream, what can you do about it? Well, first you should ride well enough to know which of the three areas—dressage, three-day, or stadium jumping—interests you the most. Then you go where the action is.

If the intricacies of dressage movements fascinate you, you might get in touch with a newly formed group called the U.S. Dressage Federation (Box 80688, Lincoln, Nebraska 68501). This organization focuses on "improving the general understanding of dressage through educational clinics, forums, and seminars." Officials work in cooperation with other horse-oriented associations, including the USET. If you're looking for dressage instruction, you can write for their "Dressage Instructor Directory," as well as for a junior membership.

"Our effort to encourage young people," says Executive Secretary Lowell Boomer, "is at this time limited to awarding the USDF Recognition for Excellence to the winning teams at the U.S. Pony Club Rallies. We've recently established the position of librarian to accumulate educational material for our members," he adds.

Frank Chapot and Main Spring.

"Another worthwhile effort is the establishment of the USDF Endowment Fund," Mr. Boomer says. "The first benefit from this endeavor comes from California, where three successful horsewomen have each been awarded $500 to defray some of their expenses while competing in the East with their eye on obtaining consideration for the United States Olympic Team."

If the grueling Three-Day Event interests you, you might turn to the U.S. Combined Training Association for help. (The USCTA is located at One Winthrop Square, Boston, Massachusetts 02110).

Neil Ayer, USCTA president (and a director of the USET as well) explains the function of his group this way. "While many of the people from the USET, the USCTA, and the American Horse Shows Association are active in several groups, the specific function of the USCTA is to support the sport of combined training. To this end, we assist in providing training for potential Olympic competitors in the equestrian Three-Day Event of the Olympic Games. We approve competitions nationally and establish procedures; we compile combined training records and statistics."

But what's combined training? According to the USCTA, "A combined training event is composed of any two competitions of the following equestrian activities: dressage, competition in the open or cross-country, and jumping. When all three activities are included, the event is popularly known as horse trials." And with good reason.

Dennis Murphy and Tuscaloosa.

If it's the big jumps that interest you, then your best avenue of approach probably lies in the major horse show circuits—shows sponsored by the AHSA. "Our present tendency is to use major existing events like the Grand Prix jumping circuit as an important part of the selection procedure," says USET head Steinkraus. In addition, many AHSA-approved shows included a USET Equitation Class that entitles high medal winners to train at the USET Training Center in Gladstone, New Jersey, home of the Jumping and Dressage teams. (The Three-Day Team is headquartered in Massachusetts.)

All right. Just suppose you gained enough experience in one of the three areas to be considered a candidate for the Olympic team. What's the final selection procedure?

Well, according to the USET, "Riders for Games squads are chosen entirely on the basis of official Pan-American or Olympic trials, conducted under the authority of the U.S. Olympic Committee. USET circuit teams are drawn from the Gladstone training squad, which consists of riders who have been invited to train under team supervision on the basis of their performance either in Games trials or USET regional screening trials."

Fine—but what are those? "Games Trials," says the USET, "are scheduled several months before each Pan-American and Olympic Games. These trials are open to anyone meeting eligibility requirements, including former team riders who may be required to compete

Bruce Davidson and Irish Cap.

in order to be considered for selection.

"Regional Screening Trials," continues the USET, "are conducted the year following each Olympic Games at various locations throughout the country. Anyone aspiring to a place on a USET training squad—either three-day or jumping—should appear at one of these trials."

Advance announcement of all these trials is made officially in the *USET News;* the AHSA publication, *Horse Show;* and the magazine, *The Chronicle of the Horse.*

Team members must be over eighteen, or over sixteen for the regional screening trials. Prospects must be U.S. citizens, and must have been certified as amateurs by the AHSA. "Women," the USET notes, "are permitted on all three squads."

Combined training, dressage tests, eventing, cross-country, stadium jumping—even the names of the competitions sound exciting. If this is your field, then dedication and training can yield untold rewards. If you're not quite that dedicated and trained, then just watching these riders in action can firm your own resolve to do the best you can in the area you're in—or just to be the best horseman or horsewoman you can be.

The United States Equestrian Team. That's something to strive for, all right. What you can accomplish depends on what you want. And on how badly you want it.

9
Horseback Holidays

By now you should be convinced that horses are definitely big business. In this country many different businesses related to horses account for a lot of paychecks. But that's not all.

Horses, as everybody knows, are for fun, too. Vacation fun. And that fun comes in almost as many varieties as there are breeds of equines. In fact, horse people themselves are something of a different breed: when they take a vacation, they may not make any attempt at all to get away from their work. Often as not, horses are as much a part of their days off as of the days on.

What do most of us think of first when we put the words *vacation* and *horse* together in the same sentence? Why, dude ranches, of course! Roundups, trail rides, impromptu rodeos, campfire sings—is there any better way to go?

Before you do go, however, you need to learn a few basic facts about dude ranches. Some may be simple family-run farms that take in occasional boarders; others are luxurious "guest ranch" spreads including everything from an eighteen-hole golf course to swimming pools—and, of course, a few horses.

Both have their advantages and disadvantages. The important thing is to know what you want before you set out.

At the family farm, for instance, you'll be able to experience country life first hand; your hosts will become your friends. But the accommodations may not be exactly Holiday Inn; you may share the bathroom with other guests—even with the host family. At the guest ranch accommodations are first class and activities are almost unlimited. But you may find yourself lost in the crowd—and your wallet will probably feel a decided pinch.

To locate the farm or ranch that suits you best, get a copy of an indispensible little paperback guidebook. *Farm, Ranch, & Countryside*

Guide is published by Farm and Ranch Vacations, Inc. (36 E. 57th St., New York, New York 10022) for $4.95, and that's money well spent. The guide covers more than five hundred recommended farms, ranches, lodges, and housekeeping cabins where vacationers are welcome. Details on rates, accommodations, and activities are included for every state in the Union and part of Canada as well.

According to guide editor Pat Dickerman, rates for a week's ranch vacation with meals range from a modest seventy dollars per person at a family-run farm to more than two hundred dollars each at a luxurious resort.

Farms and ranches are sprinkled all over the country, from Maine to Florida to California. But for a real taste of the cowboys' traditional Old West, you have to *go* West, young person!

Colorado, Montana, and Wyoming are by sheer force of number the home of the Western dude ranch. Representing more than one hundred such establishments is the Dude Ranchers' Association (Route South Laramie, Via Tie Siding, Wyoming 82084—how's that for an address?). A letter to them telling what area you're interested in will bring you a host of brochures from individual outfits. Often included are the names of previous guests who live near you; it isn't a bad idea to check with these people first to be absolutely sure you're getting the kind of place that suits you best.

Some dude ranches welcome young people alone, and so do some farms. But by and large they are, of course, a family proposition. What do you do if you're the only horse nut in the bunch? Well, you still have a lot of options, not the least of which is the summer riding camp.

Most of these are a cut above your ordinary sleep-away camp. Many specialize in teaching riding skills; some are so specialized that they concentrate only on one particular skill, like jumping, or rodeo riding. Some are for girls, some are for boys, some are coed. If you have the right information, you can match yourself up with a camp that will give you an unforgettable summer of fun and learning.

Where to find these camps? Word of mouth is good advertising, so ask around. Most Eastern organizations take ads in the Sunday *New York Times Magazine's* "Camps" section, beginning in January each year. Another good source is the American Camping Association (Rm. 810, 342 Madison Ave., New York, New York 10017). For a nominal fee they'll send you a directory of several hundred ACA-accredited camps. Again, when you write, indicate what part of the country you're interested in. The directory includes information about rates, activities, and accommodations.

What's a summer at a riding camp like? Well, you may not get much of a tan on your legs, but your face and arms will be as brown as your animal from hours of riding in the sun. Lessons are a part of every camp day, as is horse care and management. At some places each camper "owns" a special horse for the duration of the stay, and is responsible for its care.

Riding camp isn't all grueling work under the watchful eye of a ring instructor, though. Trail rides spice up the summer, and may even be held on an overnighter basis. Camps may compete against each other in intercamp horse shows; each camp sends a team and competes for most total points, or "best of show." Camp riders may attend local horse shows, too, and compete for ribbons in "the real world." Exhibitions may be held on Parents' Day, and during the regular camp session riders work to progress from one level of skill to the next. Better riders often assist beginners, and both learn in the process. (If you're a little old to attend camp as a camper, consider counseling. And see chapter 13.)

For those who are of the type or in the mood to go to one place and stay there on vacation, then dude ranching or riding camp fills the bill. But if you've got a bit of the wanderlust in you, your horseback holiday can be one of a number of exciting possibilities.

Consider, for example, the thought of traveling to the land of the horse people--to the British Isles. Mother Country to the United States, Britain is also mother to many of our horse activities. The "English" style of riding, Pony Club, fox hunting, steeplechase, dressage, three-day events--all these came to us from England. If you want to trip to the land of our equine origins, many options are open.

Like pony trekking. Listen to this, from the British Tourist Authority: "In these days of fast, efficient transport, leisurely pony trekking is becoming increasingly popular. Daily treks [trips] are made on horseback, from centres often based in beautiful countryside, through scenery unaccessible by any other means than on foot. Often covering rugged moorland and mountain, the treks are necessarily conducted at a walking pace and are therefore suitable for a beginner. More experienced riders will be given the opportunity of trotting and cantering."

Strike your fancy? A letter to the BTA (680 Fifth Ave., New York, New York 10019) and a visit to your local travel agency or AAA will set your mind to wandering. Also available in England are visits to such famous racetracks as Ascot and Epsom; "riding holidays" at various equestrian centers located throughout the country; and even fox-hunting in season.

In neighboring Ireland, an extra flavoring is added to the horse holiday: caravanning! Caravanning? Well, listen to the Irish Tourist Board:

Beginning riders receive some sound instruction on untacking from an old Scotsman at the end of their ride. *Courtesy British Tourist Authority.*

"Ireland is one of the few countries in Europe which is suitable for horse-drawn caravanning, as many of our roads are comparatively free from heavy motor traffic. This form of holiday is definitely not the thing for anyone in a hurry. It is a leisurely affair. You will probably travel no more than 15 kilometres (about 10 miles) per day.

"But that, of course, is the beauty of horse-drawn caravanning: You have time to appreciate the countryside, to see places and things you would not otherwise notice, time to meet people who will stop to chat with you and exchange views on this, that, and the other."

The caravans themselves look like tiny barns on wheels, and are equipped inside much like a camper, with cooking facilities and berths for four people.

"Your silent companion, the horse, has been chosen with care for his task," the Tourist Board continues. "A short period of instruction at the base before you depart, on harnessing and unharnessing and horse care, will give you the necessary confidence to look after your horse. Specially selected routes to give you variety and suitable overnight stopping places will be part of your briefing and then you are off on your holiday.

"Time often stands still in Ireland and the unpredictable is a

Let's go pony trekking in England! Here riders of all sizes and talents enjoy the rolling countryside of Perthshire from the backs of their sturdy and complacent little animals. *Courtesy British Tourist Authority.*

British pony-trekking expeditions include rolling hills and quiet forests—places you could hardly expect to see through the window of a tour bus. *Courtesy British Tourist Authority.*

These are Irish caravans—little round houses on wheels which enable
you to sample the real Irish countryside at your leisure, at a horse's
pace. What better way to get a good, close feel of what Ireland is really
like? *Courtesy Irish Tourist Board.*

specialty. You will make many new friends and finish your holiday
with regret at leaving but with a real desire to return to a friendly and
hospitable people."

Before you start packing your bags, however, shoot off a letter to the
Irish Tourist Board (590 Fifth Ave., New York, New York 10036).
They'll send you names and addresses of caravanning outfits, and give
you other basic information.

For instance, an Irish caravanning holiday costs about twenty-five
dollars per day per person (minimum four); the charge includes the
caravan, all cutlery and cooking utensils, sheets and blankets, gas,
mattresses, and "a healthy, willing horse." Most caravan companies also
offer rental of riding horses with their caravans, for a nominal
additional fee.

Sounds great, doesn't it? Pony-trekking across England, caravanning
through Ireland. . . But maybe your wanderlust has a wide imagination

and a somewhat thinner wallet. What then? Well, within the confines of the United States lots of possibilities are still open to people who want horses in their holidays.

Perhaps one of the best-known of these is a program called Trail Riders of the Wilderness, sponsored by the American Forestry Association (1319 18th St. N.W., Washington, D.C. 20036). Spring Flower Rides and Fall Color Rides are offered in the Great Smoky Mountains of North Carolina and Tennessee; a battery of wilderness rides take place in different parts of the West. Cost ranges from two hundred dollars to five hundred dollars per person for six to eleven days, and you bring your own equipment (sleeping bag and mattress, boots, clothing, etc.) You don't have to carry it with you, though; packstock is provided.

Here's a description of just one of the Western tours, to give you an

In County Galway, Ireland, visitors stop for a chat with grazing Connemara ponies on a country road. *Courtesy Irish Tourist Board.*

Riders take to the trails at the Kentucky State Horse Park near Lexington, the only park to be dedicated solely to the horse. A former Thoroughbred stud farm, the Horse Park now features a wide variety of horse-related activities. *Courtesy Kentucky State Development Cabinet.*

idea of what the Trail Riders are all about—and to whet your appetite. The scene is the North Cascades mountains in Washington state.

"The snow-capped peaks of the Northwest present some of the most gorgeous scenery anywhere. From three camps, there are numerous side trip opportunities to jewel-like lakes and streams for fishing or bathing; or to flower-laden alpine meadows, dense forests, and towering peaks. Watch for marmots darting among the rocks; as well as ptarmigan; you may also see a cattle drive in progress. A ride to the Canadian border presents a sweeping view, and from atop Sheep Mountain there is a panorama of the Pasayten Wilderness and Mt. Baker." This particular trip costs $390 from the base camp at Winthrop, Washington; it lasts nine days.

A caution to young people who might want to attempt such a ride alone is offered by Mary Ellen Walsh, director of the Trail Riders of the Wilderness.

"We do not get into youth activities as such," she says, "but many young people do participate in our rides with their families. Youths are permitted to go on any of our trips with adult companions, which can be parents or some relative or even a family friend if authorized by the parents."

Other groups, however, *do* offer trips especially tailored for kids. To find out what's available you need a copy of the *Adventure Trip Guide. 1,000 Selected Vacations Ideas,* available from Adventure Guides, Inc. (36 E. 57th St., New York, New York 10022). How does a coed pack trip strike you, for instance? Cattle and horse drives? A class in mountain horsemanship? All the information is in the guide. And you'd do well to check out the chapter called "For Teens and Up." Also, the groups described in the final chapter, "With Other Adventurers," very often include young people in their plans.

Still another possibility for those of you traveling with your families is horseback riding in our National Park System. Private operators,

Trail riders enjoy the rolling Bluegrass scenery of the Kentucky State Horse Park. Miles of board fencing and open pasture are typical of the entire Lexington area. *Courtesy Kentucky State Development Cabinet.*

stables, and ranches offer riding trips in most parks, both state and national. Just look around! For a few bucks an hour you can see parts of the parks that most visitors never imagine are there! Some parks, of course, offer more extensive facilities than others; at one place you may get an hour's ride around the campground, while somewhere else may be able to set you up for an overnight pack trip. But you'll never know unless you ask!

One park, however, stands out as the place all horse people should know about. Located in what is possibly the horsiest state in the country, the brand-new Kentucky State Horse Park near Lexington scheduled completion in July 1976. Formerly the Walnut Hill Stud Farm, the new park offers a flurry of activities and attractions guaranteed to pull in horse lovers from everywhere.

Plans for the horse park include a visitors' activity complex with an orientation and information center, museum and theater, gift and craft shops, picnic area, petting zoo, equestrian events, and pony rings. The steeplechase course is a flat one-mile track with both brush and timber jumps. In addition, there's horseback riding (of course!) on trails that wind throughout the Model Farm area. Old-fashioned horse-drawn carriages are available, too, to take nonriding visitors around the Farm.

So go somewhere this year! Light a fire under your family. Go to Kentucky, go West, go to England, go riding! But go!

10
Equine Environmentalists

The uninitiated eye may see horse people in general the way Stephen Leacock once described one: "He flung himself from the room, flung himself on his horse, and rode madly off in all directions."

We'd probably be a little less than honest if we didn't admit that such behavior probably applies to all of us at one time or another. But it surely isn't true of most people most of the time. Horsemen have a special contact with the outdoors. What happens to wilderness and to wildlife directly affects the horse community, for instance. And as the horse world is diverse, so are the environmental concerns of its people.

Take the plight of the wild mustang, for example. After years of being hunted by helicopter and chopped up into dog food, these horses were placed under the care of the federal Bureau of Land Management when Congress passed the "Wild and Free-Roaming Horses and Burros Act" of 1971. But the danger is far from passed.

The some twenty-thousand mustangs that still roam free on government lands are in trouble. They're still harassed by airplane roundups, still shot for sport, and still run off their lands by stock operators looking for more grazing room for their own profitable cattle businesses. Horse people have risen up in a body to protest.

The mustangs' plight was pinpointed in Idaho, when a group of wild horses were rounded up and treated in a manner not even fit for dog food.

An article from the *Washington Post* was read into the Congressional Record. It begins, "Ranchers slit the throats of some of the wild horses they drove to the edge of a cliff near Howe, Idaho, and cut their legs off with a chain saw."

Outraged horsemen formed into groups to take the case of the wild horses to the courts and to the people. The American Horse Protection Association (3316 N St. N.W., Washington, D.C. 20007) rounded up its

Here at the base of a cliff in a remote area of Central Idaho, lie wild horses who were apparently stampeded over the edge to their deaths. These horses are the center of a raging court battle between friends of the wild horses, the Bureau of Land Management, and ranchers. *Courtesy F. L. Dantzler, Humane Society of the U.S.*

One group of several wild horses found at the bottom of the cliff in the Idaho mountains. Note the use of "hog rings" in the nose of the center horse. These metal, staplelike clamps were inserted to cut off breathing and thus make the animals more manageable. *Courtesy F.L. Dantzler, Humane Society of the U.S.*

six thousand members in an emergency appeal to save the survivors of the Idaho slaughter.

The Association warned, "When Clark Gable, against the protests of Marilyn Monroe, set out in 'The Misfits' to trap mustangs for dog meat, the film was widely regarded as allegorical, a symbol of the dying days of the Wild West. But reality, as so often in America, has a habit of imitating art."

Under the leadership of Mrs. William Blue, the AHPA began a series of court appeals and injunctions. Senators and movie stars enlisted in the wild horse cause. Lorne Greene, formerly of the television show "Bonanza," shared a press conference with the AHPA horse mascot across from the White House.

Amanda Blake of "Gunsmoke" fame joined with another group called Wild Horse Organized Assistance, or WHOA! (P.O. Box 555, Reno, Nevada 89504). Led by another crusader named "Wild Horse

Survivors of the Idaho "massacre" await their fate in an Idaho stockyard. *Courtesy Wild Horse Organized Assistance.*

Some months after their ordeal, these same mustangs have fattened up and even dropped a few foals. The original purpose of the "roundup" was to sell these animals for dog food. *Courtesy F.L. Dantzler, Humane Society of the U.S.*

Annie" Johnston, WHOA! dedicated itself wholly to the preservation of "the wild ones." WHOA! members went along as observers on government-sponsored "harvests" of so-called "excess animals." They, too, file suits for protection of the mustangs. And whenever possible, they secure animals who can't be returned to the wild and place them out for "adoption" by WHOA! members.

"Our participation in the fight for survival of the wild horses and burros," WHOA! says, "includes surveillance to assure their safety and well-being. Constant vigilance must be maintained in the vast unsettled and remote areas of the West to guard against and to report infractions of state and federal laws for the protection, management, and control of wild free-roaming horses and burros. In order to carry out its commitment to vigilance, WHOA! has volunteer observers throughout the Western states."

Anxious to prevent another Idaho fiasco, mustang protection groups have undertaken to find "adoptive homes" for mustangs the Bureau of Land Management decrees must be removed from their ranges. This frisky foal is one of sixteen removed from a mountain range when it was feared they faced starvation. *Courtesy Wild Horse Organized Assistance.*

Members of these horse protection groups are often young, and always committed. A "Pencil War" waged by youth, in fact, was a prime mover in the original passage of the Horse and Burros Act by Congress. A junior riding club in Arizona took on an emergency fund-raising operation they called HAY—Havasupai Assistance by Youth—in order to get feed to a group of starving Indian ponies on a Grand Canyon reservation. Two thirteen-year-olds in Massachusetts staged a "People for Horses Show" where the ribbons were lettered SAVE THE MUSTANGS HORSE SHOW and a mustang's head centered the rosette. Proceeds went to WHOA! to further the group's activities.

The AHPA has a youth group of its own—the Junior American Horse Protection Association. AHPA says the junior club was established to "bring the parent organization's vigorous education program into the homes and classrooms of children between the ages of 6 and 16. The AHPA is convinced that cruelty to animals is committed for one of two reasons: ignorance and/or greed. Therefore, it is our goal to educate younger Americans to value and respect all living creatures."

In this the AHPA has made great strides. The organization led the battle for the passage of the Horse Protection Act in Congress, which outlaws "soring," a brutal training method inflicted on Tennessee Walking Horses. The AHPA joined with WHOA! and other groups to press for passage of the act, and it also investigates horse shows, substandard riding stables, horse auctions, horse farms, or any other place where horses are mistreated. Legal action is initiated where necessary.

Membership fees in these organizations are nominal, and include newsletters, bulletins, and opportunities to purchase occasional specialty items like pins and stationery.

Also involved in decent treatment of horses by people are the humane societies. The American Humane Association (P.O. Box 2788, Denver, Colorado 80201) is the nation's first and largest humane federation. The AHA concerns itself with child welfare and child abuse, in addition to offering various services to about twelve hundred different animal agencies. The association inspects animal perform-ances—including rodeos and horse shows—and is also involved with the protection of endangered species like the mustang and with the care of livestock. The AHA sponsors the PATSY (Performing Animal Top Star of the Year) Awards you may have seen on television, and is equally concerned with the innocent abuse many "backyard horses" receive due to the ignorance of their owners.

An offshoot of the AHA is the Humane Society of the United States. HSUS has its national headquarters in Washington, D.C. (2100 L St. N.W., zip code 20037) as do other protection agencies. Its intent is broader in scope, however, and its interest in horses is an extension of its desire to "prevent cruelty to all animals, from household pets to exotic wildlife." This group carries a big stick in the horse world, and has plenty of clout.

According to a publication titled *Respect for Life*, "The Humane Society of the United States is not the only national humane organization, but its members believe it is the most progressive in terms of nationwide change in inhumane practices and attitudes. It is especially active in working with members of Congress to draft humane legislation and in taking court action to stop inhumane practices by agencies of the government. Whenever possible, HSUS bands together with other organizations in the fields of animal welfare, conservation, and ecology to attack problems of common interest."

In the case of the wild mustangs, HSUS joined hands with AHPA against the Bureau of Land Management over the Idaho "dog food roundup." Frank L. Dantzler, director of the West Coast Regional Office of HSUS, visited the roundup site and called the event "the most outrageous incident of animal cruelty I've seen in 10 years of humane society work."

Infuriated by the treatment these horses had received, Dantzler told newsmen that none of the animals found dead at the base of the cliff were shod or branded. "There are indications," he added, "that in the fury and excitement of the roundup, the animals nearest the edge likely stampeded over the rocky side from fear."

All this activity from all these organizations secured the Idaho mustangs at least temporary respite, and placed the whole Horse Protection Act in serious legal jeopardy when ranchers rose up in a body to protest.

Once again the horse lovers were incensed. And another load of work has been placed on the friends of "the wild ones."

At the HSUS, horses are the center of yet another battle—between the Society and rodeo at large. This is less a legal fight and more a public row, and tempers flare on both sides.

Briefly, the HSUS claims that rodeo events, roping in particular, are cruel and inhumane and should be stopped altogether. The group urges its members to protest rodeos in their own communities by informing local humane societies and local officials of HSUS' study.

According to HSUS, "An investigatory study of rodeo roping events conducted for HSUS has found that in calf roping, a 225-pound calf is usually traveling at approximately 27 miles per hour at the moment it is lassoed. The resulting force exerted on the calf's body is enough to injure the calf, sometimes severely."

The Rodeo Cowboys Association calls the HSUS report "not factual" and "dealing in generalities." The RCA maintains it has "never denied that rodeo is a rough competitive sport," but claims that more physical damage is done annually to the cowboys themselves than to the rodeo stock.

The furor arose over the introduction of two bills into the Colorado Legislature designed to ban roping and busting (slamming to the ground) of any animal in rodeos. The HSUS president maintained in hearings that "There are no events in rodeo performances that are more injurious to calves and steers than those events employing the act of roping." He added, "The blatant nature of these events should convince any sensitive person that animals so roped are being subjected to torment, pain, and injury."

The RCA retorted with disdain. To the hearing room packed with rodeo supporters, the RCA stated that rodeo is not cruel. "It can be a dangerous sport," the RCA officials admitted; "injuries to both contestants and animals do occur on occasion but such injuries are unintentional, accidental, and regrettable. Dangerous sports and cruel sports are not synonymous."

The RCA went on to cite dollars and cents. "The economics of injured animals alone prevents rodeo people from intentionally injuring the stock. For example, a calf that might be injured when it is roped can be harder to handle and tie than an uninjured one. And with calves selling for around $200 each and steers going for $300 under current price trends, a stock contractor would soon be out of business if he had a lot of injured stock."

The argument has not ended. It rages through all of rodeo. The use of flank straps on bucking horses and bulls, veterinary treatment or lack of it—even the existence of rodeo itself is at issue.

"One of the most disturbing aspects of rodeo," says the HSUS, "is that it gives children who participate an insensitive outlook on animals. Through Little Britches rodeo groups, high school rodeo groups, and collegiate rodeo associations, children and youth are taught to treat animals inhumanely in the name of competition. Such an atmosphere of violence may be psychologically damaging to children."

But, claims the RCA with some pride, "At least a third of our active professional membership has had previous experience in junior, high school, and college rodeo ranks." The main purpose of these groups is to teach sportsmanship and citizenship to young people.

Who's right? Well, you'll have to make up your mind. But a definite controversy exists.

Horse people are concerned about horse use, whether the animals be wild or domestic. And they're concerned about land use, too—the two million acres occupied by their eight million horses.

The National Horse and Pony Youth Activities Council (affiliated with the USDA Extension Service) has made some suggestions and proposals concerning zoning and land as relating to horses.

A recent Council report admits, "The tremendous growth of the horse industry causes problems in almost every community. Families call City Hall asking, 'May we keep a horse in our backyard or adjacent lot?' 'Where can we ride?' 'Where can we have horse shows?' On the other hand, complaints are made relating to safety, odor, flies, cleanliness, noise, and dust."

Local zoning boards, the report suggests, "have the responsibility of arriving at agreements which meet the needs of the entire community. Their function should not," the Council warns, "be that of just controlling or limiting horse owners. They must find ways to settle differences and establish regulations which satisfy non-horse owners, yet do not severely limit the recreational benefits of horsemen." The report, available from the Council, is titled "Guidelines for Horsemen and their Communities: Zoning." A companion paper is "Horses and Land-Use Planning."

As horse people we want the best for our animals, and for ourselves. Your position in any controversy over horses should be well researched, well thought out, and then well executed. Mere opinions, whether on the fate of mustangs, or rodeo, or of your own backyard pasture, mean nothing unless they're accompanied by concrete action.

11
Schools for Young Riders

When you reach a certain level of proficiency in a sport, any sport, you naturally begin to consider the possibility of "turning pro." Am I good enough, you wonder, to earn a living doing this? Do I know enough about what's involved to know whether I want to do it on a fulltime basis? And what can I expect from a sports career, anyhow?

When you begin to ask yourself these questions about the horse business, you're getting into serious territory. A person doesn't go out and set up a riding stable, or hang out a shingle as a trainer, or hire out as a show rider, on good intentions alone. You have to have ability, and you have to have training.

In the horse world there are two main routes you can take toward a solid career education. Both require completion of high school. You can attend one of several horsemanship career schools located across the country, and be certified by that school. (In the United States we have no national equestrian certification, as England does.) Or you can choose to go on to a college offering degrees in horse science—but more about that in the next chapter. Let's look at the career schools first.

Say, for example, that you're nearing the end of high school and you want to get into a horse-related career as soon as possible. You opt for the practical training of a career school, and chose to pass up college. Now what?

First, get hold of all the bulletins you can find from these schools. (Most advertise regularly in the monthly horse publications.) Study the literature carefully. Compare costs, total course time, distance from home, facilities, and special course offerings.

Then look at yourself again. Just what sort of career do you want? Are you really set on an area of specialization? If you are, then matching yourself to a suitable school shouldn't be too difficult. But if you're still unsure what you want to specialize in, you should look for a school that offers as many different options as possible.

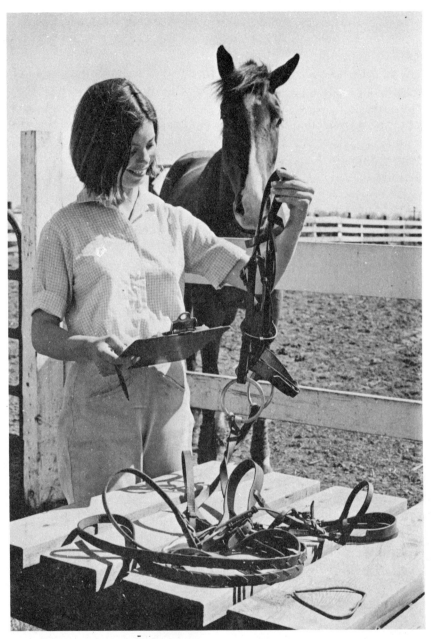

Students at Pacific Horse Center—and all the other career horsemanship schools—learn as much about horses on the ground as they do topside. Here a student studies parts of tack. She'll also learn to repair and clean bridles, saddles, and a host of other horse paraphernalia. *Courtesy Pacific Horse Center.*

In any case, visit the schools that interest you most. Inquire about scholarships, if finances are low; many places offer a "working student" arrangement whereby you exchange barn work for room and board.

Finally, you choose. What sort of life can you expect to lead for the next few months?

Well, let's take a close look at a few of these schools. For the sake of geographical coverage we'll examine one in the West, one in the Midsouth, and two in the East. Many other schools exist, of course; this is by no means a complete list. But the ones we'll discuss—Pacific Horse Center in California, Huntlea Horse Center in Tennessee, Potomac Horse Center in Maryland, and Morven Park International Equestrian Institute in Virginia—will give you a good idea of what's available, and what to expect.

First, though, a few facts are basic to most of the career schools. Fees are inclusive—that is, they cover room, board, horses, and instruction. Most places have facilities where students may bring their own horses if they wish (at additional expense for boarding). Most

At Pacific Horse Center in California, students line up for instruction at the beginning of one of their two daily riding sessions. *Courtesy Pacific Horse Center.*

A student at Pacific Horse Center negotiates a jump under the watchful eyes of his instructor and fellow students. *Courtesy Pacific Horse Center.*

schools don't take anyone under about sixteen; some require a high school diploma. Instruction is divided between practical and theoretical, and between class, barn, and riding ring.

Most schools don't accept rank beginners; they are, after all, concentrating on career training, so they expect students to know something about the field they intend to enter. But this doesn't mean that you have to be a top-notch rider to be accepted. All most places ask is that you be capable of riding comfortably at all three gaits, and perhaps be able to take small jumps. You should be both physically fit and mentally enthusiastic. And you really must love horses, because you'll be literally breathing and sleeping horse lore during your course of study.

Now, let's start in the West and work our way East. The Pacific Horse Center is located near Sacramento, California; mailing address is Box L, Elk Grove, California 95624. Two major courses of study are available: the introductory Horsemastership (Assistant Instructor) and

Advanced Horsemastership (Instructor). Both run for three months each. Cost of the first course is $1,800; the advanced course is $2,000.

The Horsemastership Course is, according to the Center, "designed for those who wish to broaden their knowledge and improve their techniques, either from a desire to enter more advanced competitions, because they intend to make their career with horses in the fields of training, teaching, or management, or simply for their own pleasure and personal satisfaction."

The course is a comprehensive study of the theory and practice of hunter seat equitation, with twice-daily riding sessions, lectures, demonstrations, and field trips. Graduates of this basic course should, the Center says, "be capable of taking charge of a small stable or acting as an assistant to the manager of a larger one; they are also capable of teaching at beginner level, and of acting as an assistant instructor at a more advanced stage."

The advanced course at Pacific is designed for those who wish to remain at the school after completing the basic course, and prepare for specialized riding at a more advanced level.

"Students follow the framework of the basic routine at the school. However, they are given the freedom to specialize in the particular field

A Huntlea student practices an exercise to deepen her seat as she's lunged by her instructor. *Photo by Harriet Hatchell, courtesy Huntlea Horse Center.*

of equestrian study most interesting to them. Students in this course,"
the Center explains, "are assigned two horses. One is a carefully
selected horse to care for and show in competition. The other is a green
horse to care for and train under the personal supervision of the Chief
Instructor. Thus the students acquire a complete understanding not
only of training technique but also of the preparation, conditioning,
and feeding of horses for competitions."

As at most career horsemanship schools, the Pacific Horse Center
staff actively assists graduates in finding jobs. Positions such as assistant
trainer, instructor, stable manager, and professional rider are often
available. In addition, both courses are worth six credits each at
California State University in Sacramento. Students don't have to be
attending college at the same time, and the credits are fully transferable
to any other accredited college or university in the country.

Huntlea Horse Center in Waco-Lynnville, Tennessee (zip code 38472)
offers instruction in both Western and English riding styles. Huntlea
courses consist of Horsemanship Phase I (Assistant Instructor), which
covers the basics of equitation, stable management, minor ailments, and
principles of instruction; Horsemanship Phase II, covering advanced

Sidesaddle classes have been recently added to the curriculum at
Huntlea. *Photo by Harriet Hatchell, courtesy Huntlea Horse Center.*

Huntlea students perform the Wheel in an English drill. *Photo by Harriet Hatchell, courtesy Huntlea Horse Center.*

riding and theory; and Horsemastership (Graduate), which specializes in the finer points of instructing, showing, and eventing. Inclusive cost for each course is $1,700. Huntlea offers a "thorough 15-week school, well-balanced in training and horsemanship." Students receive practical experience in driving, sidesaddle, eventing, and fox hunting (Huntlea shares acreage with a hunt for which one of the co-owners is Senior Whipper-In). In addition, extracurricular activities include horse shows, visits to breeding and training barns, and combined training events.

Huntlea students may be novices, eventers, owners, or career candidates. The school has no age limit, but does require a high school diploma. Huntlea features its own breeding program in which students participate in the care of mares and foals, and in the training of young horses as well.

Moving farther East, we encounter career schools that are often larger, fancier, and more British. The Potomac Horse Center (Rt. 3, Gaithersburg, Maryland 20760) boasts over one thousand acres of land in the heart of hunt country. This establishment has not one but two indoor riding halls, stabling under a single roof for one hundred horses, and such other incidentals as jumping and dressage arenas and a huge cross-country course. Here the main instructors are certified by the prestigious British Horse Society.

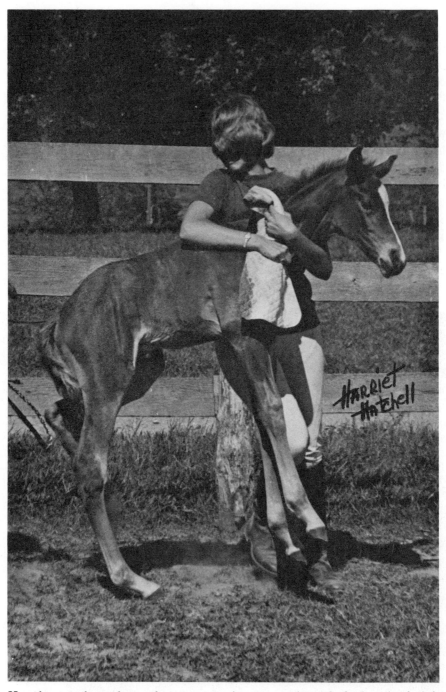

Huntlea students have the opportunity to work with foals raised right at the school. Looks like this girl's got quite a handful! *Photo by Harriet Hatchell, courtesy Huntlea Horse Center.*

As at the other schools, Potomac divides its courses into levels. "These courses are designed to educate those who wish to become riders, trainers, instructors, stable managers, and jockeys, by producing people who are capable of either taking charge of a small establishment, or being the efficient assistant to the manager of a larger one," says Potomac. "The instructional staff strives to create a stimulus in the students to further their knowledge and to extend their ability in whichever field their interests lie, be it in dressage, jumping, eventing, hunting, veterinary science, or stable management, or racing; and to develop in them sound teaching techniques in order that they may, in turn, pass on their knowledge to other students."

The basic course at Potomac is the Training Certificate, or Course I. Students work for three months to learn basic dressage and jumping, and are taught the rudiments of instructing and stable management. "Students holding this certificate will be well equipped to become a camp instructor or to hold a similar position," according to Potomac.

A student at Potomac jumps in exhibition in one of the indoor arenas. *Courtesy Potomac Horse Center.*

Students tone up their cross-country jumping skills on this difficult downhill multiple obstacle at Potomac. *Courtesy Potomac Horse Center.*

The Training Certificate also readies a student to undertake the more difficult Horsemasters Course; applicants here "should be able to walk, trot, canter, and jump a course of 2'6" fences before applying."

The Horsemasters Course here is taught in two three-month segments. Part I encompasses equitation, stable management, and teaching, but is primarily devoted to "the development of the rider, strengthening the seat, and improving the style. Competitions are organized from time to time so that students can compete among themselves."

Part II students find their instruction "directed more to the training and schooling of the horse, starting with lungeing and long-reining a young horse and going on to training and preparing a young horse for showing, eventing, jumping, etc. Students will have lessons on the more advanced horses and will be expected to compete among themselves in a One-Day Event covering dressage, cross-country, and stadium jumping. As the student progresses he will be given a horse to school on his own, for a period during which time he must accomplish whatever project his instructor has set for him." Or her.

Total cost for the Training Certificate course is $1,300; as at the other schools, the price is inclusive. The Horsemasters Course in its six-month, two-part version costs $3,250, but total payment isn't required all at once. Half is made at the beginning. Then, Potomac says, "At the end of the eighth week, the student will be advised either to complete the whole six-month course or only take the first three months. Some students need a little more time and mileage; therefore, we suggest they find a job as an assistant or, if they prefer, they can stay at the Potomac Horse Center as working students until they are ready for the last three months of the Horsemasters Course."

The second Eastern school is also near the nation's capital, this time in Virginia. Like Potomac, the instructors are British. Like Pacific, the equestrian courses count toward college credit. Like Huntlea, the

The end of a long day. Potomac students discuss their work and their animals as they prepare to leave the spacious barn. *Courtesy Potomac Horse Center.*

students must be high school graduates. But Morven Park International Equestrian Institute is in many ways very different from any other career horsemanship school.

For starters, Morven Park (Rt. 2, Box 8, Leesburg, Virginia 22075) is a twelve-hundred-acre estate and the former home of a former governor of Virginia, Westmoreland Davis. The Westmoreland Davis Foundation now owns the estate, and opens the historic mansion and boxwood gardens to the public and, among other programs, operates a carriage museum on the grounds. The Equestrian Institute was established here by the United States Combined Training Association (USCTA) with the Foundation's assistance; recently the Foundation has taken over management and the USCTA uses the grounds for trials.

Morven Park offers only one course of study that lasts nine months. The Equitation Instructor's Course is fully residential (as are the other

Horse and rider take the fence in style as the stately Westmoreland Davis mansion looks on. The occasion? Dedication day for Morven Park. *Courtesy Morven Park International Equestrian Institute.*

schools); cost for board, room, and study for the entire stay is $5,750, or about $2,700 for each of two semesters.

Here a preenrollment interview is not only suggested, it's required, along with a "ride" by the prospective student to determine ability. Only then, and only accompanied by character references and a medical certificate, is a student accepted for study.

"Instruction at the Institute," says British Army Major Jeremy Beale, the chief instructor, "is based upon a general utility or balanced seat, which enables the rider to hunt, show jump, steeplechase, perform dressage, and school horses, with only a slight variation in length of stirrup. Our aim," he says, "is to produce riders who are poised, confident, and relaxed, and who demonstrate complete harmony and understanding with their horses."

Course work at Morven Park is divided into riding (twice daily), stable management, veterinary, first aid, and teaching. Students here have the unique opportunity of taking complete charge of a class for a full week, under the direction and supervision of the school staff. Frequent lectures by a local veterinarian are "designed to study the horse as a biologic entity."

Morven Park students have access to horses of outstanding quality, including some retired veterans of international competition. Horses as well as riders are accepted as "recruits," and both undergo the same sort of rigorous training.

Emphasis during the fall semester is placed on improving the student as a rider; in the second semester ability to instruct is stressed. By the time graduation rolls around in the spring, students have earned the right to wear the Morven Park uniform: bottle-green coat with emblem, and buff breeches.

And, along with the graduates of career horsemanship schools throughout the country, they've acquired a solid backgrounding that will eventually enable them to command top salaries in all kinds of horse industry positions.

12

Horses Go to College

You say you want a career with horses, friend, but your parents want you to go to college? You say you want the mental exercise of college, but your true love lies with horses? You say horses and college don't mix—or your parents say it?

Well, take a walk in the sun! Horses and college *do* go together. And the variety of mixes offer you the sort of education you want with horses and the sort you want from college, too. You *can* have it both ways.

All over the country colleges and universities are very heavily into horse-related programs. Some institutions offer only a class or two, some an area of specialization, some a degree in horse science (see Appendix II, a list of colleges offering horses courses, compiled by the American Horse Council).

In this chapter we'll look at two such schools, each with a different method of combining horses with higher education. One is a land-grant university in the heart of Kentucky Bluegrass-Thoroughbred country; the other is a cooperative venture between a career horsemanship school and a private college. Neither program is totally unique in itself; each produces graduates with horse knowledge and book learning, too.

At the University of Kentucky in Lexington, students take equitation and horse husbandry classes on the grounds of the University-owned Maine Chance Farm, a former race-horse spread once held by Elizabeth Arden. Guest speakers in even the introductory classes come from some of the largest Thoroughbred breeding farms in the country, if not the world. (The renowned Calumet Farm, with its miles of white fence and small city of red-trimmed white barns, lies just across from the Lexington airport.)

According to Dr. John Baker, who heads the University's horse

The spacious grounds of the former Maine Chance Farm in Lexington now provides housing for horses involved in the University of Kentucky's horse science program. *Courtesy University of Kentucky.*

program, "Horse courses are taught in the Department of Animal Sciences within the College of Agriculture. Thus, students graduating within the horse area receive a Bachelor of Sciences degree in Agriculture with a minor in Animal Sciences and a specialty in horses."

The degree itself may sound complicated, but it's nothing to what students who earn it will learn. "I'm constantly advising students to take math and chemistry courses, for one thing," Dr. Baker says. "How can you learn about equine nutrition without chemistry, or about genetics without math? Not impossible, but we want our students to be fully grounded in their area of study."

If you were to decide on the University of Kentucky, what would you be getting into, coursewise? Well, first you'd register in the College of Agriculture (and you'd be surprised at the number of young women who do). Then you'd be assigned to the Animal Production departmental major, and would be signed up for such courses as these: Fundamentals of Animal Nutrition; Live Animal and Carcass Evaluation; Animal Science Seminar; Animal Breeding; Reproduction and Artificial Insemination in Farm Animals.

In the course of your four years you'd take a smattering of classes in math, chemistry, and biology, and probably some electives in the College of Arts and Sciences. And you would, of course, get what you came for: a thorough education in horse science.

You'd take Introductory Horse Husbandry, where you'd learn the basics of breeds, feeding, disease control, management practices, and elementary horsemanship theory. You'd take Farrier Principles & Practices, which would give you anatomy of horse hooves and legs, with

USCTA Director Kob Ryen teaches an equitation class on the grounds of the University of Kentucky's Maine Chance Farm. *Courtesy University of Kentucky.*

Aerial view of Meredith Manor, which in conjunction with a local college offers a baccalaureate degree in Horse Studies. *Courtesy Meredith Manor School of Horsemanship.*

emphasis on corrective hoof trimming and proper shoeing.

More advanced courses include Horse Science, which goes into much greater detail on subjects related to horse production, training, and farm management. The Advanced Horse Husbandry class would give you information on housing facilities for horses, agronomic practices, and economics and marketing. In addition, students from the advanced class are assigned, in pairs, the care and training of one of the University's horses on the Maine Chance Farm for a full semester.

And you'd take riding courses. Beginning and intermediate equitation, jumping, dressage, and equitation teaching are all taught by Kob Ryen, a Norwegian whose qualifications include membership on the Board of Directors of the U.S. Combined Training Association.

Well. Sounds like when you get out of U.K., you'd be ready to take over Calumet Farms single-handed. Right?

Wrong. Dr. Baker cautions prospective students, and his advice holds true for anyone considering a horse career.

"Many people," Dr. Baker says, "make the mistake of thinking that they'll be fully qualified to be trainers or barn managers or whatever as soon as they graduate. They won't be. While students do emerge with a sound, well-rounded knowledge of horses and horse management, their practical experience is still to come. And we can't teach horse sense in the class room—it has to be learned in the School of Hard Knocks."

In other words, folks, even college graduates have to start at the beginning and muck out stalls.

For those who wish to further their educations beyond the bachelor level, U.K. has a fully active master's and Ph.D. program, including what Dr. Baker calls "the most active equine nutrition graduate program in the country."

Kentucky is the place to go for almost any kind of horse activity. And Lexington is the center of everything. Two racetracks feature both flat and harness racing; there's an active Hunt Club; the largest outdoor horse show in the country is held here; and best of all, there are plenty of people around who talk and understand Horse. Whether the course of study at U.K. is right for you, though, is for you alone to decide.

Not far away, in Waverly, West Virginia, is a very different breed of horse-and-college program. Here, thanks to the collaboration of a career horsemanship school called Meredith Manor and small Salem College, students can earn a Bachelor of Science Degree in Equestrian Studies in three years.

Meredith Manor also offers nondegree courses that are very similar in content and cost to the courses described for other schools in the preceding chapter. But here the thirty-six-week Riding Master course may be combined with two years of liberal arts study at Salem College. With a little luck and a lot of study, a baccalaureate degree results.

Students interested in the combined program may complete its requirements in several different ways. Either the two-year college program may be completed first, then the Riding Master course, or the college program may be alternated with the Three Summers Program, which divides the Riding Master course into three twelve-week periods offered for three consecutive summers.

Degree candidates at Meredith Manor have the option of choosing a major in either English or Western riding, or a double major that includes them both. In addition, Riding Master candidates choose an area of emphasis—riding, training, or teaching. Thus each student can zero in on the course of study most interesting to him or her, and the staff can in turn offer emphasis where it's most wanted.

The Riding Master course counts for half the credits necessary for

Meredith Manor students can major in English or Western riding as they study, or they can choose a double major, which combines both styles. *Courtesy Meredith Manor School of Horsemanship.*

At Salem College, a program has been worked out with nearby Meredith Manor School of horsemanship that allows students to combine their undergraduate liberal arts studies with a practical career training in horsemanship. *Courtesy Meredith Manor School of Horsemanship.*

the bachelor's degree, and is divided into three quarters (or three summers, depending). Each quarter includes classes in riding, training, stable management, teaching techniques, judging, and showmanship. Those who complete the basic studies of the first quarter are elegible for Meredith Manor's Camp Instructor certificate. The second quarter course continues the program on a more advanced level; graduates here earn the Riding Instructor certificate.

By the time Meredith Manor students reach the third quarter of study, they will have worked extensively on their own ability as riders and trainers of young horses. They'll have competed in school horse shows, and assisted with riding lesson programs (including day camp in the summer). During this last quarter the emphasis shifts. Students are now introduced to dynamics as it relates to horsemanship. They're responsible for training a colt, and they undertake a study of the economics and general management of a horse operation. They have practical experience in planning and giving riding lessons, and in judging school horse shows. And they enter into an advanced program of horse show competition.

The courses taken at Salem College, which count for the other half of the necessary credits for the bachelor's degree, are divided into general areas. Included are Communication Skills, Man and His Universe (sciences), Man and His Civilization (arts and languages), Man and His Society (economics and history), and Man and His Home (consumerism, phys. ed., etc.). Students elect a specified number of credits in each area to complete their general liberal arts education.

All students at Meredith Manor, whether enrolled in the degree program or not, are required to have completed high school satisfactorily, although occasionally students headed for the degree are admitted to the Three Summers Program while still in high school. (Applicants must be at least sixteen, however.) Like the other career schools, Meredith Manor assists graduates with job placement, and follows up on their professional employment after graduation.

So you see, it *can* be done. And a lot of colleges are doing it. The demand is growing for qualified, trained horse people as the industry expands. And educators are moving to satisfy that goal. You don't have to go to the University of Kentucky or to Meredith Manor to get a college education for a horse career—opportunity is nationwide.

Your interest and participation will keep it that way.

13

Getting a Job
in the Horse Industry

Recession, inflation and economic downturn notwithstanding, the horse industry is growing faster than a long-legged colt. In size, in stature, in financial impact. And as more horses appear on the scene, so the need increases for more people to work with those horses.

Are you one of today's young horse people who's headed for a lifelong equine career? Would you be happy in the horse industry? And what opportunities are available to you, anyhow?

The questions are easier to ask than they are to answer. Dixon D. Hubbard, head of the USDA's Horse Industry Advisory Council, says, "A large number of seemingly well-trained young people are continuously contacting my office as well as the American Horse Council, horse breed associations, and other horse industry organizations, relative to possible employment in the horse industry. We all feel that employment is available, but none of us seems to be able to specifically identify where, or to effectively guide potential employees to their potential employers."

Which drops the horse career problem almost squarely in your own lap. Because although the industry is aware of the communications gap and is gradually gearing up to meet it (the National Horse and Pony Youth Activities Council has a guideline on employment for young people in the horse industry now underway), advances are slow and coordination between the widely different elements is difficult.

So your interest in a horse career is likely to be yours alone. Are you really the kind of horseman or horsewoman who'd be satisfied with a lifelong business association with horses, or are you better off maintaining your pleasure-rider status?

The prime prerequisite anyone who aspires to a horse career must have is guts—and a strong willingness to do whatever has to be done, including mucking out stalls. No employer wants a know-it-all recruit who's afraid of getting dirty. *Courtesy Pacific Horse Center.*

Look at a few of the main considerations.

First, and most important to many horse industry employers, is this: Would you be as willing to muck out stalls and to clean tack as you are to ride?

Indeed, this seems to be the chief bone of contention among established horse people. Most of them consider the young people who seek horse careers to be well-grounded in basic horsemanship skills; many would-be trainees, in fact, boast excellent backgrounds. They just don't want to work around the south end of a northbound horse.

More than one owner of a small horse establishment has complained to me about the difficulties they've had in finding people—whom they desperately need—who are prepared to take the bitter with the sweet, or the shovel with the saddle. As one woman put it, "All my applicants wanted a salary at minimum wage and no stall or other 'dirty' work. They wanted only the benefits of horse ownership without any of the expense and work—and then they wanted to be paid, too!"

Naturally she was steamed. And so are many of her confederates. With the need for boarding and riding stables increasing so rapidly, these owners are crying for good help. But they need *help*, not the burden of another "expert" around the barn who's afraid of dirty boots.

These small stables, incidentally, are excellent training grounds for horse careers. You can get almost any kind of specialized training you want, plus basic practical experience that will prove invaluable when you're ready to move up the career ladder or out on your own. And best of all, you can probably find such a place right in your own neighborhood that needs you right now—no matter what your age!

But you must be willing to work, and work hard. Horsekeeping is hard work, and lots of it. Besides being beautiful and a whole lot of fun, horses are also messy, very apt to get sick, and in need of all kinds of equipment that must also be properly cared for.

Before you apply for a job at that local stable, then, be sure you want to learn as well as earn—and that you're willing to put in hard work for solid experience. If you find you want the fun of horses without the problems, then stick to renting your mounts at riding stables, or boarding your own animal at a boarding stable. Just don't go to work there yourself.

All right. Nuff sed. If you think you'd be more than willing to put in long hours at not-so-glamorous jobs in order to secure your life with horses, then you're on the track.

Another point you ought to consider is pay. Although there certainly are a lot of people in the horse industry with a lot of cash, the fact remains that most of the underlings who do most of the work don't exactly get rich quick—if at all.

Our source of financial information is Charles Hunt, owner of Huntlea Horse Center in Tennessee (see chapter 11). He advises his own graduates about job placement and replies to several hundred employment inquiries a month, so he needs to know what he's talking about. With him, we'll outline job possibilities and the average going pay scale for each position.

Let's take breeding farms first. Jobs for beginners are often available with mares, foals, and weanlings, and may include fitting yearlings for auction sales (teaching manners and quieting), as well as foaling watch over pregnant mares. "Pay averages $90 to $100 per week plus room," Mr. Hunt says. "Trainees can advance eventually to Broodmare Manager. Here the pay is $150 to $250 a week, and usually includes a house and other side benefits." Mr. Hunt suggests Thoroughbred and Standardbred farms as offering some of the best job opportunities.

Many jobs for beginning horsemen are available in the racing field. Here one man acts as "hot walker" for a horse who's already been worked, while two others are exercise riders. *Courtesy Keeneland Association.*

An exercise rider takes an early-morning gallop. The amount of money he can make in a day depends on the number of "rides" he can rustle up. *Courtesy Keeneland Association.*

Then come the breeding-racing farms. "Grooms breaking yearlings to saddle and exercising them earn $75 to $90 per week. Riders earn about $90; they may also act as grooms or work with broodmares and yearlings."

At racing-training stables, grooms muck out stalls, bed down horses, feed and water, tack up and untack, and cool out horses for $90 to $100 a week plus, perhaps, a share of any track winnings. "Exercise riders," Mr. Hunt says, "usually earn about $3.50 per 15-minute ride, and may ride four to eight horses daily, depending on the size of the stable. These riders may also pony entries at races; for $5.00 per race they lead the horse and jockey to the starting gate. Grooms," Mr. Hunt adds, "usually take the horse to the saddling paddock before a race and return him to the barn after the race is through. This carries a fee, too."

Hot walkers do just that: they walk the horses to cool and calm them after exercise or a race. Hot walking, according to Mr. Hunt, pays about $2.50 an hour, although some stables prefer to pay by the horse.

All horse industry jobs aren't in the racing world, of course. If you aspire to responsibility and are capable of bossing both people and animals, then you can head for a career as a Barn Manager. You might work for a racing stable, but you could also seek work at hack and boarding stables, club stables, hunts, and breeding farms. "Pay for a barn manager is from $150 a week up," says Mr. Hunt, "and usually includes a free house. In return, you're in charge of all barn employees, and have full responsibility for all the horses in the barn." Not a job for a beginner, but certainly one worth setting your sights on.

Or perhaps you'd like to be a trainer. What's your specialty—hunter-jumper, racing, gaited, Western, driving? As a full-fledged trainer you'll earn upwards of $150 a week plus house, purses, or bonus. As an Assistant Trainer you're more or less apprenticed to an experienced person for on-the-job learning; cash money may be no more than $50 to $125 per week, but an apprentice to a good trainer gains much more than a paycheck. A trainer who sets up in business may work on a fee-per-horse basis, and is likely to maintain his or her own establishment. "Income depends on reputation and success," Mr. Hunt warns, so you should be both well grounded and well known before attempting to strike out on your own.

Want to be a riding instructor? A good place to start is at a summer riding camp. Fees aren't much—perhaps $500 for two months, plus room and board. But here again, the experience is what counts. You work with all kinds of kids at all levels of skill—and you meet up with all kinds of horses, too. Becoming a riding counselor is an excellent way to get a taste of the real world of horses, and an idea about how your

This girl could be headed toward a career training jumpers, as she learns to lunge an unmounted horse over obstacles. *Courtesy Pacific Horse Center.*

own career plans should proceed. My own experience with camp counseling placed me in an excellent position: under an adult Riding Master. Most young people aren't quite ready to assume total responsibility for a stable full of horses and a camp full of kids.

If you can still live with the combination of kids on horses after your summer of counseling (I personally had a terrific time), then you can start looking for full-time work as a Riding Instructor at a teaching stable.

"Usually a six-day week is involved," Mr. Hunt says. "Pay scales differ widely depending on the size and type of stable, but I'd guess average income to be about $100 to $125 per week plus room or room and board. Pay may either be on straight salary, or on base wage plus commission, or on straight commission (a percentage of the price charged to each student you teach). Reputation, experience, and publicity also contribute to income. Schools and colleges," he adds, "pay about $5,000 per year plus room and board for yourself and your own horse. Salaries can range up to about $8,000 annually."

If your own horsemanship is top-notch, if you've won consistently in large horse shows and are well known in horsey circles, and if your prime interest in horses is riding, then you might consider turning pro. "Show riders on the gaited and hunter-jumper circuits may be paid expenses plus all of won purses," says Mr. Hunt. "Another method is base wage plus a certain percentage of any winning purses as bonus."

All of these careers relate directly to the riding and immediate care of horses. But jobs in the horse industry are practically unlimited, and allow for all different kinds of talent.

If you've a head for business you might run a tack shop or deal in riding apparel. Horse people with a knack for words can seek out jobs as reporters on horse-oriented newspapers and magazines, or do free-lance writing and publicity. You can do office work for a farm or a stable; you can become a horse show organizer. You can sell feed. You can be a horse photographer. Make saddles. Shoe horses. Learn auctioneering. In short, whatever you do well is probably of use in the world of horses. With a little ingenuity you can bring almost any specialized skill into its own in the horse industry.

Still another avenue of approach to horse careers is down the road of veterinary medicine. The best basic information on all kinds of veterinary careers, from equine practitioner to veterinary assistant to equine research specialist, is available from the American Veterinary Medical Association (600 South Michigan Ave., Chicago, Illinois 60605).

Want to be a vet? Well, be prepared, the association says, for at least six years of college study before you earn that D.V.M. or V.M.D. degree. And then you have to pass a state board exam before you can be licensed to practice anywhere. (See Appendix IV for a list furnished by the Association of Colleges of Veterinary Medicine.)

If you dream of being a horse doctor then you'd better change your tune—today they're called equine practitioners, and they have their own specialized American Association of Equine Practitioners (Route 5, 14 Hillcrest Circle, Golden, Colorado 80401).

This group defines an equine practitioner as "a Doctor of Veterinary Medicine who specializes in equine medicine and surgery and other equine medical services. His basic professional education is the same as that of other veterinarians. Specialization comes after graduation from veterinary college, by graduate and post-graduate studies, informal internship, practice, and application."

"Some," the association continues, "specialize their practices to meet the needs of breeding farms, Thoroughbred and Standardbred racing, horse shows, other equestrian events, and specific breeds of horses. Others specialize in a specific discipline such as equine surgery, radiology, or nutrition. The majority, however, engage in general equine practice, servicing all breeds of horses and all types of medical problems."

If you're not prepared to undertake quite so much study, vocational careers are also possible as veterinary assistants and with veterinary drug houses.

In short, then, careers in the horse industry are as many and as varied as the people who fill them. I've by no means covered all the possibilities; I've merely taken a quick look at some of the opportunities.

The horse industry in the United States is a relatively new phenomenon, and one still in a state of rapid growth and change. So what it boils down to is this: if you have the desire to make a go of horses as your life's work, then you also have the chance to carve your own niche just to suit you.

The field is wide open.

14

Prognosis for

the Prodigal Horse

What's the outlook for the horse industry of tomorrow? For the horse himself? For horse people? To look intelligently at the future, we first should glance at the past.

Without the horse to take us from one coast to the other, our history would be very different. Even our boundaries might have been different, for reaching the West—and holding it once we got there—would have been a whole other story.

This country was founded from the backs of its horses. From Paul Revere's race through Massachusetts to the mad dash for gold in California, horses have been vital to the making of American history. They settled the East, they opened the West, and they farmed the country's rich midland.

As the human population grew, so did the horse population. In 1920, the number of horses peaked at an all-time high of twenty-six million head. But then the automobile came into being. The mechanical revolution began in earnest. And gradually horses faded from the scene. By 1959 only three million animals were left—so few that the USDA quit counting them.

By this time mechanization and computerization were established as The Way of Life. So was hurry and bustle, urbanization, and increased leisure time. Strangely enough, these were the very elements that set the stage once again.

Caught in the crush of modern living, people began to rediscover horses. Not the heavy-duty, multipurpose animal of years gone by, though—now the horse was considered a thing of beauty and an animal of pleasure. Riding off into the sunset was about to become a national pastime.

Dr. Dixon D. Hubbard of the Horse Industry Advisory Council (USDA) explains it this way. "Today's horse is a horse of a different size and with a different purpose than the draft horse of the past. It's the light horse which has ascended to these new heights, because he is a key figure for a recreation-minded people with more money to spend and more leisure time in which to spend it than any population in horse history. Riding for pleasure, in shows, hunts, rodeos, attending the races, or participating in other horse events became marks of distinction among Americans in the 1960's."

The pleasure horse population began to climb—and with it began a sudden proliferation of all sorts of horse-related organizations and industries, all intent on the struggle to keep abreast of the nation's new spectator and participant sport.

For people weren't content to watch other people at the races, at horse shows, and at rodeos—they wanted horses for themselves. And so did their kids—which led to the phenomenal increases in youth horse activity.

In short, horses lost little time in regaining their place of importance in American life. Horses are indeed big business again.

Small-time saddle clubs dominate the landscape from coast to coast. Big-time racing stables turn over more money in a year than do many school systems. Even the government is in the horse business in a big way, from 4-H to USDA Horse Specialists to the National Horse and Pony Youth Activities Council. And looking over the government's shoulder is the horse-interest lobby led by the American Horse Council.

But where do we go from here? Horses have shown phenomenal growth in all areas of equine activity. Is this growth a good thing? Is it likely to continue? And what are the implications of a booming equine population rate in today's world?

Judging from the rapid recent rise of horse-related groups and associations, I think it's safe to say that horse people in the know see their industry as one on the rise, despite national tendencies to moan over the state of the world in general.

In fact, the horse industry, because it *is* a pleasure and leisure industry, may even benefit from such periods of national gloom. To be sure, people may not be in the market for the extremely fine and expensive horses. But those who can afford to ride may do so more often, as a means of escaping from the pressures of the workday world.

In any case, horse people seem to be scrambling over one another to get to the new crop of novices, and to provide goods and services needed by novices and professionals alike. Expansion in this industry, in fact, just can't keep pace with the demand.

Take the field of horse information, for example. Most of our horses

The future of the horse industry depends on its youngest riders—like my daughter, who at six has already been riding two years. What these kids lack in length of leg they make up in strength of voice—and the horse world had better watch out!

are pleasure animals, and most are owned by just plain folks. "The popularity of the horse among inexperienced pleasure horse owners," Dr. Hubbard says, "has opened a large market for information on horsemanship and horse management. This market is currently flooded by more misinformation based on fads and fancies than has been seen in any other livestock field. Also, supplementing the poor information is the prevailing market for 'training gimmicks.'

"The magnitude of the horse industry and enrollment in 4-H horse projects have expanded so rapidly," he concludes, "that it has been difficult to keep pace with the increased demand for education and service associated with this rapid growth."

While 4-H may have started the ball rolling, other organizations were quick to jump on the bandwagon. Most of the youth divisions weren't formed until the 1960s, and even the now-presitigous American Horse Council didn't come into being until 1969. Since then, though, everyone's been struggling to make up for lost time.

According to the AHC, "The increase in horse numbers was accompanied by an equally sizeable increase in the number of horse owners. These people were in need of education and services relating to the production, management, care, and use of their horses. The demand far exceeded the supply of both information and people to service the industry.

"Also," the AHC points out, "the needs of the new light horse industry are considerably different from the old draft horse industry. These horses are light-boned horses, a different type and temperament than draft horses, used not for work per se, but for sport and recreation. Consequently, previously existing research information obtained from studies on draft animals wasn't applicable."

So horse research has been stepped up. More interest is now being shown in the fields of equine health and nutrition—the American Association of Equine Practitioners jumped its membership from one hundred to one thousand horse veterinarians in less than ten years!

Colleges are now into the act, too. Physical education courses in horsemanship have been spruced up and beefed up. Horsemanship training now includes much more than a basic knowledge of how to get on and off the animal and how to stay on once up.

Agricultural colleges have combed their people for horse knowledge, and have set up horse science courses and degrees. Then along came the riding camps, the horsemanship career schools, and all the other training groups.

But, says the AHC, "The horseman of the 1970's does not necessarily have a prior knowledge of the correct care, feeding, management, health, and general welfare of the horse, as was once handed down from generation to generation by his forefathers for whom the horse was an agricultural necessity."

The country's horse population doubled in the 1960s, and estimates for 1980 go up to fourteen million or more. So while there's no doubt about the growth of the horse world, and little doubt that the growth will continue, there is some question about how beneficial the increase has been.

In any industry with such a rapid growth rate, problems are likely to develop quickly. Novice horse owners, for instance, mean accidents to animals and to people. Do you know how much damage can result when half a ton of loose horse meets three tons of moving automobile, head on? Have you ever been the victim of a well-meaning but uninformed motorist who gaily tooted his horn at you and spooked your mount well into the next county?

A young rider works hard, away from the summer sun, as she strives toward perfection in her chosen sport. On her, and on so many others like her, the future of the horse rests.

The problems of the horse industry—and dissemination of information is one of the most pressing—rest in the hands of horsemen, young and old. For horses have once again taken their rightful place in our economy, in our world, in our lives. The USDA Extension Service sees it this way:

"Horses are generating tax revenue, helping meet recreational needs, serving agriculture, and most important of all, helping in the development of youth.

"Concurrently, they are stimulating the economy of businesses selling horse supplies and equipment, such as feed, tack, facilities, and clothing, as well as transportation, lodging, and restaurants.

"Also, more trainers, horsemen, farm managers, field service and breed association personnel, feed company employees, Extension personnel, researchers, teachers of equitation and horse science, farriers, veterinarians, and many others are needed to service this expanding industry."

There you have it, folks. The horse is here to stay. But the quality of his future—and of your future as a horseman—depends on you. On your interest in perfecting your own skills, and on your desire to expand your knowledge and influence beyond your own pasture fence.

The prodigal horse has indeed returned to open arms. As a horse lover, you have a vital stake in the continuing health of his industry.

Appendix I

The following is a list of equestrian facilities throughout the country that have conformed to certain standards set up by the Riding Establishment Committee of the *American Horse Shows Association,* and operate with the approval of the Association. A list of these establishments, and the facilities and programs they offer individually, is available upon request, without charge, by contacting the Association office, *527 Madison Avenue, New York, NY 10022* Tel. 212-759-3071.

AUBURN FARMS, INC.: Robert E. Latinville, 231 E. Main St., Georgetown, MA

BARRINGTON HILLS RIDING CENTER: Mr. John C. Arnold, Bateman Road, Barrington, IL 60010

BEAR RIDGE RIDING CLUB: Mrs. Judy Barta, 594 Bear Ridge Rd., Pleasantville, New York 10570

BONNYBROOK FARMS: Mr. & Mrs. Jos. Mercuri, 2020 E. Spring Valley Rd., Spring Valley, OH 45370

BREEZY HILL MORGANS: Loran & Patricia Sheley, Littleton, NH 03561

CAMP BOBBIN HOLLOW: Mrs. W. Henry Sr., Bay Rd., Amherst, MA.

CANNONS POINT HUNT STABLES: Mr. Drue Linton, P.O. Box 665, Lawrence Rd., St. Simons Island, GA 31522

CATAMOUNT HUNT CLUB, INC.: Charles W. Ackerman, 336 Haverstraw Rd., Suffern, NY 10901

CEDAR CREEK STABLES: Diane L. Morgan, 3900 Hursh Rd., Ft. Wayne, IN 46825

CHERRY MEADOW FARM SCHOOL OF HORSEMANSHIP: Mrs. Dorothy P. Sachey, 1072 Pulaski Rd., East Northport, NY 11731

CORY WALKEY TRAINING CENTER: Miss Cory S. Walkey, 1881 Old Topanga Canyon Rd., Topanga, CA 90290

CQ STABLES: Jack E. Coughlin, 142 Holbrook Drive, San Antonio, TX 78218

CUB HILL RIDING SCHOOL, INC.: Carroll L. Herbert, 10301 Harford Rd., Glen Arm, MD 21057

DUNMOVEN FARMS, INC.: Clifford Hunt, Dark Hollow Rd., Box 144, Wycombe, PA 18980

EQUINE EDUCATION CENTER: Mr. & Mrs. Donn and June Adams, 12222 143rd St., Orland Park, IL 60462

5-H ACRES SCHOOL OF RIDING: Mrs. Samuel A. Hendrickson, Kinney Gulf Rd., Route 4, Courtlandt, NY 13045

FOXFIELD RIDING SCHOOL: Mrs. Wm. O. Postel, P.O. Box 570, Westlake Village, CA 91360

FOXHILL SCHOOL OF HORSEMAN-SHIP: Mr. Ed Treifler, Greenfield Park, NY 12435

FOXTAIL FARM: Mrs. Jan Shephard, Box 323, Coursegold, CA

FRANCES REKOR SCHOOL OF HORSEMANSHIP: Mrs. Frances F. Rekor, Happy Horse Stables, Rockford, MN 55373

FRANMERYL FARM: Doris Fee, RD 2, Featherbed La., Ballston Spa, NY 12020

FULL CRY FARM: Nancy S. Lane, 2225 McMullen Booth Rd., Clearwater, FL 33515

GLENBURN VALLEY FARM: Mr. Gordon W. Spencer, Canal Road R.D. 1, Princeton, NJ 08540

GRANDVIEW STABLES, INC.: Mr. & Mrs. A.W. Renihan, Jr., 1005 W. 64th St., Indianapolis, IN 46260

GREENWAY EQUITATION SCHOOL: Mildred F. Gaines, Greenway, VA 22067

HERITAGE FARM: Jerry Raucher, 30 Florence Rd., Easthampton, MA

HICKORY HILL HORSE HAVEN ARABIANS: Barbara A. Giordano, 94 Mill Plain Road, Branford, CT 06405

HIDE-A-WAY FARM: Mr. & Mrs. F. Cort Clifford, Rt. 2, Box 96, Sykesville, MD 21784

HILLAIRE RIDING CLUB: Mrs. H.O. Bilby & Mrs. G.L. Doolittle, Hillaire Circle, White Plains, NY 10605

HILLCROFT ACRES SCHOOL OF RIDING: Mrs. Louise S. McConnell, 6340 McIntyre St., Golden, CO 80401

HOLLOW HAVEN FARM & SCHOOL OF HORSEMANSHIP: Keith D. Bartz, 8411 Great Plains Blvd., Chanhassen, MN 55317

HOLLY HILL STABLES: Mr. & Mrs. Donald S. Harter, P.O. Box 293, Arbita Springs, LA 70420

HULL PRAIRIE CLUB: Dr. George D. Black, 26981 West River Rd., Perrysburg, OH 43551.

HURDLE HILL FARM: John T. Shaffner, 7310 Chesnut Ridge Rd., Lockport, NY

JUNIOR EQUITATION SCHOOL: Jane Marshall Dillon, 9710 Clark Crossing Road, Vienna, VA 22180

KAALEA VIEW FARM R.A. INC.: Mrs. Jack L. Tugman, Jr., 47-744 Lamaula Pl., Kanohe, HI 96744

KNOLL FARM OF SUFFOLK CITY: Mr. David L. Cribbons, 849 Suffolk Ave., Brentwood, NY 11717

KOKOHEAD STABLES, INC.: Mr. Frederick G. Harting, III, P.O. 7526, Honolulu, HI 96821

LITTLE ACRES RIDING STABLE: Mrs. Ralph M. McNeal, RD 4, Landing Neck, Easton, MD 21601

LITTLE HOPE RANCH, INC.: Mr. Robert C. Wideman, Route 1, Box 263, Conyers, GA 30207

LOCHILL FARM: Bill Gosling, RT 1, Box 204, Hillsborough, NC 27278

MAR-VISTA RIDING ACADEMY: Mrs. Dev Terrill, 2152 Skyline Blvd., Daly City, CA 94105

MEREDITH MANOR: Mr. Ronald W. Meredith, Route 1, Box 76, Waverly, WV 26184

MERRYMOUNT HORSE CENTER: Mr. & Mrs. C. Dersin, R.R. Box 4106, Frank Tippett Rd., Upper Marlboro, MD 20870

MID-ACRES FARM: Col. John W. Russell, 5529 Vance Jackson, San Antonio, TX 78230

MIDLAND RIDING CENTER: Mr. B.G. Hardaway, III, P.O. Box 1360, Columbus, GA 31902

MILES RIVER RIDING SCHOOL: Mrs. G.W. Barner, Route 1, Box 578, Easton, MD

MONTRESOR: Mr. Neal A. Stanford, Route 2, Box 33, Leesburg, VA 22075

MORGAN'S SCHOOL OF RIDING: Mrs. Nola K. Morgan, 2188 Lester Rd., Valley City, OH 44280

MT. HOLYOKE COLLEGE STABLES: Mr. John Moffat, Mount Holyoke College, South Hadley, MA 01075

MOUNTAIN VALLEY EQUESTRIAN CENTER: Richard L. Villa, E. Flat Hill Rd., South Britain, CT 06487

OAK MANOR SCHOOL: Mrs. Theodosia S. Berry, Route 1, Box 265, Weyers Cove, VA 24486

OPEN GATE FARM: Rhoda Joan Hopkins, Hanover Rd., Newtown, CT 06470

PACIFIC HORSE CENTER: Mr. Lawrence Langer, P.O. Box L, Elk Grove, CA 95624

PATCONG CREEK FARM: Joyce E. Schiereck, Box 229, C RD 2, Pleasantville, NJ 08232

PEGASUS-MEADOWBROOK STABLES: Mr. James H. Little, Meadbrook Lane, Chevy Chase, MD 20015

PLEASANT HOLLOW FARMS: Mrs. John C. Cory, Box 481, R.D. 1, Coopersburg, PA 18036

POTOMAC HORSE CENTER: Mr. Frederick B. Harting, Jr., 14211 Quince Orchard Road, Gaithersburg, MD 20760

RED FOX STABLES: Mr. Lawrence R. Smith, 1342 State Route 50, Milford, OH 45150

RED RAIDER CAMPS: Mr. Ralston Fox Smith, 20800 Almar Dr., Shaker Heights, OH 44122

RICE FARMS: Mr. Frank Rice, Box 44, Huntington, NY 11734

RICHARDSON STABLES: Mr. L.D. Richardson, RR 3, Box 67-A Heckel Road, Evansville, IN

RIDGEVIEW STABLES: Lois Heyerdahl, 7263 Ridgeview Rd., La Crosse, WI 54601

ROUND HILL STABLES, INC.: Theodore F. Wahl, Pecksland Rd., Greenwich, CT

RYEGATE STABLES: Roy E. Reneker, Richard Snelbaker, RD 2, Mechanicsburg, PA 17055

SADDLE RIVER RIDING CLUB: Henry F. Hulick, So. Nelson Rd., Sterling Junction, MA 01565

SADDLEWOOD FARMS: George J. Higgins, P.O. Box 658, Covington, LA 70433

SHALLOWBROOK EQUESTRIAN CENTER: Mr. Hal A. Vita, Sr., Hall Hill Road, Somers, CT 06071

SHENANDOAH FARMS RIDING SCHOOL: Altheia P. Clarkson, Rt. 5 Box 110, Staunton, VA 24401.

SOMERSET CO. PARK COMM. RIDING STABLE: Henry O. Chase, 256 So. Maple Ave., Basking Ridge, NJ

SOUTHERN SEMINARY JUNIOR COLLEGE STABLE: Bernard W. Gaiser, Jr., P.O. Box 300, Buena Vista, VA 24416

SOUTHLANDS RIDING SCHOOL: Mrs. Gregory Thomas, Southlands, Rhinebeck, NY 12572

SPRUCELANDS RIDING CENTER: Mrs. Sheldon Black, Sprucelands, Java Center, NY 14082

THE STABLE: John Cully, Jr., R.D. 5, Brinton Bridge, Rd., West Chester, PA 19380

SULLINS COLLEGE: Barbara Hatcher, Dept. Head., Virginia Park, Bristol, VA 24595

SWEET BRIAR COLLEGE RIDING CENTER: Mr. Paul D. Cronin, Sweet Briar, VA 24595

TRAVELERS REST ARABIANS: Mrs. Margaret Dickinson Fleming, Rt. 7, Pulaski Pike, Columbia, TN

VANTAGE POINT FARM: Ron E. Palelek, Vantage, WA 98950

WATERFALL FARM & STABLE: Paul Okolowicz, Spring Valley Rd., Ridgefield, CT 06877

WINFIELD MANOR, Cynthia Everett, Rt. 1, Box 101, Fargo, ND 58102

WINDY HILL FARM: Mrs. Charlotte S. Malkin, Amity Road, Bethany, CT 06525

ZODIAC FARM: Dr. & Mrs. P.E. Whittlesey, 4650 South Hampton Rd., Dallas, TX 75232

Appendix II

American *Albino* Association, Inc.
Box 79
Crabtree, Oregon 97335

Andalusian Horse Registry of the
Americas
c/o Mrs. H. Clawson
Center Island, Oyster Bay, New York
11771

Appaloosa Horse Club, Inc.
P.O. Box 8403
Moscow, Idaho 83843

National *Appaloosa Pony,* Inc.
Box 297
Rochester, Indiana 46975

Arabian Horse Registry of America, Inc.
One Executive Park
7801 East Belleview Avenue
Englewood, Colorado 80110

The *Half-Arabian* Registry and *Anglo-Arab* Registry
International Arabian Horse Association
224 East Olive Avenue
Burbank, California 91503

American *Bashkir Curly* Registry
Box 453
Ely, Nevada 89301

American *Bay* Horse Registry
P.O. Box 790
Bend, Oregon 97701

Belgian Draft Horse Corporation of
America
P.O. Box 335
Wabash, Indiana 46992

American *Buckskin* Registry Associ-
ation
P.O. Box 1125
Anderson, California 96007

International *Buckskin* Horse Associ-
ation
P.O. Box 357
St. John, Indiana 46373

Cleveland Bay Society of America
White Post, Virginia 22663

Clydesdale Breeders of the United
States
Route 3
Waverly, Iowa 50677

American *Connemara Pony* Society
HoshieKon Farm
Goshen, Connecticut 06756

American *Crossbred Pony* Registry
P.O. Box 202
Newton, New Jersey 07860

American *Donkey* and *Mule* Society,
Inc.
2410 Executive Drive
Indianapolis, Indiana 46241

Galiceno Horse Breeders Association, Inc.
111 E. Elm Street
Tyler, Texas 75701

Gliding Horse & Pony Registry
19100 Beat Creek Road
Los Gatos, California 95030

American *Gotland* Horse Association
R.R. 2, Box 181
Elkland, Missouri 65644

American *Hackney* Horse Society
P.O. Box 630
Peekskill, New York 10566

American *Indian* Horse Registry, Inc.
Rocking LJK Ranch
Route 2, Box 127
Apache Jct., Arizona 85220

Standard *Jack & Jennet* Registry of
America
Route 7 - Todds Road
Lexington, Kentucky 40502

Royal International *Lippizzaner*
Club of America
Route 7
Columbia, Tennessee 38401

The American *Miniature* Horse Registry
P.O. Box 468
Fowler, Indiana 47944

Missouri Fox Trotting Horse Breed
Association, Inc.
P.O. Box 637
Ava, Missouri 65608

Morab Horse Registry of America
P.O. Box 143
Clovis, California 93612

American *Morgan* Horse Association
P.O. Box 265
Hamilton, New York 13346

American *Mustang* Association, Inc.
P.O. Box 122
Berling, Wisconsin 54923

American *Paint* Horse Association
P.O. Box 13486
Fort Worth, Texas 76118

The *Palomino* Horse Association, Inc.
P.O. Box 324
Jefferson City, Missouri 65101

Palomino Horse Breeders of America
P.O. Box 249
Mineral Wells, Texas 76067

American *Part-Blooded* Horse Registry
4120 SE River Drive
Portland, Oregon 97222

Paso Fino Owners & Breeders
Association, Inc.
Suite 605, Blount Professional Building
Knoxville, Tennessee 37920

American *Paso Fino* Horse
Association, Inc.
Room 3018
525 William Penn Place
Pittsburgh, Pennsylvania 15219

Percheron Horse Association of
America
Route 1
Belmont, Ohio 43718

American Association of Owners &
Breeders of *Peruvian Paso* Horses
P.O. Box 371
Calabasas, California 91302

The *Pinto* Horse Association of
America, Inc.
P.O. Box 3984
San Diego, California 92103

Pony of the Americas Club
1452 N. Federal, Box 1447
Mason City, Iowa 50401

American *Quarter Horse* Association
P.O. Box 200
Amarillo, Texas 79168

Original *Half Quarter Horse* Registry
Hubbard, Oregon 97032

Standard *Quarter Horse*
4390 Fenton
Denver, Colorado 80212

Colorado Ranger Horse Association
(Rangerbred)
7023 Eden Mill Road
Woodbine, Maryland 21797

American *Saddle Horse* Breeders
Association
929 South Fourth Street
Louisville, Kentucky 40203

The *Half Saddlebred* Registry
of America
660 Poplar Street
Cochocton, Ohio 43812

Shetland Pony Registry
1108 Jackson Street
Omaha, Nebraska 68102

American *Shetland Pony* Registry
P.O. Box 468
Fowler, Indiana 47944

American *Shire* Horse Association
Box 19
Pingree, Idaho 83262

Spanish-Barb Breeders Association
P.O. Box 7479
Colorado Springs, Colorado 80907

The *Spanish Mustang* Registry, Inc.
Route 2, Box 74
Marshall, Texas 75670

The United States Trotting Association
(Standardbred)
750 Michigan Avenue
Columbus, Ohio 43215

American *Suffolk* Horse Association
672 Polk Boulevard
Des Moines, Iowa 50312

Tennessee Walking Horse Breeders'
and Exhibitors' Association
P.O. Box 286
Lewisburg, Tennessee 37091

The Jockey Club *(Thoroughbred)*
300 Park Avenue
New York, New York 10022

Half-Thoroughbred Registry
c/o American Remount
Association, Inc.
P.O. Box 1066
Perris, California 92370

Trakehner Breed Association & Registry
of America, Inc.
Route 1, Box 177
Petersburg, Virginia 23803

American *Trakehner* Association
Norman, Oklahoma 73069

National Trotting & Pacing Association,
Inc. *(Trottingbred)*
575 Broadway
Hanover, Pennsylvania 17331

New Jersey *Trotting Bred Pony*
Registry
P.O. Box 202
Newton, New Jersey 07860

American *Walking Pony* Association
Registry
Route 5, Box 88
Upper River Road
Macon, Georgia 31201

Welsh Pony Society of America
Drawer A
White Post, Virginia 22663

Appendix III

Universities and colleges offering equine courses:

University of Arizona—Tucson, Arizona

Arizona State University—Tempe, Arizona

Prescott College—Prescott, Arizona

Scottsdale Community College—Scottsdale, Arizona

University of Arkansas—Fayetteville, Arkansas

Arkansas State University—State University, Arkansas

Auburn University—Auburn, Alabama

University of California—Davis, California

California State Polytechnic University —Pomona, California

California State Polytechnic University —San Luis Obispo, California

California State University—Chico, California

Fresno State College—Fresno, California

Clemson University—Clemson, South Carolina

Colorado State University—Fort Collins, Colorado

Lamar Community College—Lamar, Colorado

University of Connecticut—Storrs, Connecticut

University of Delaware—Newark, Delaware

Delaware Technical & Community College, Northern Branch—Wilmington, Delaware

University of Florida, Gainesville, Florida

Santa Fe Community College—Gainesville, Florida

University of Georgia—Athens, Georgia

University of Idaho—Moscow, Idaho

University of Illinois, Urbana, Illinois

Belleville Area College—Belleville, Illinois

Purdue University—Lafayette, Indiana

Ball State University—Muncie, Indiana

Iowa State University—Ames, Iowa

Kirkwood Community College—Cedar Rapids, Iowa

Kansas State University—Manhattan, Kansas

University of Kentucky—Lexington, Kentucky

Murray State University—Murray, Kentucky

Morehead State University—Morehead, Kentucky

Louisiana State University—Baton Rouge, Louisiana

Louisiana Polytechnic Institute—Ruston, Louisiana

McNeese State College—Lake Charles, Louisiana

Southeastern Louisiana University—Hammond, Louisiana

University of Maine—Orono, Maine

University of Maryland—College Park, Maryland

University of Massachusetts—Amherst, Massachusetts

Mt. Holyoke College—South Hadley, Massachusetts

Cheff Center—Augusta, Michigan

Michigan State University—East Lansing, Michigan

University of Minnesota Technical College—Crookston, Minnesota

University of Minnesota—Waseca, Minnesota

Mississippi State University—State College, Mississippi

University of Missouri—Columbia, Missouri

Lindenwood College—St. Charles, Missouri

Stephens College—Columbia, Missouri

Williams Woods College—Fulton, Missouri

Montana State University—Bozeman, Montana

University of Nebraska—Lincoln, Nebraska

University of New Hampshire—Durham, New Hampshire

Centenary College—Hackettstown, New Jersey

Rutgers University—New Brunswick, New Jersey

Cazenovia College—Cazenovia, New York

Cornell University—Ithaca, New York

State University of New York,—Alfred, Canton, Cobeskill, Delhii, and Morrisville Campuses

North Carolina State University—Raleigh, North Carolina

North Dakota State University—Fargo, North Dakota

Ohio State University—Columbus, Ohio

Lake Erie College—Painesville, Ohio

Oklahoma State University—Stillwater, Oklahoma

Eastern Oklahoma State College—Wilburton, Oklahoma

Northwestern State College—Alva, Oklahoma

Panhandle State College—Goodwell, Oklahoma

Oregon State University—Corvallis, Oregon

Pennsylvania State University—University Park, Pennsylvania

University of Rhode Island—Kingston, Rhode Island

South Dakota State University—Brookings, South Dakota

Black Hills State College—Spearfish, South Dakota

University of Tennessee—Knoxville, Tennessee

Middle Tennessee State University—Murfreesboro, Tennessee

Texas A & M University—College Station, Texas

West Texas State University—Canyon, Texas

University of Vermont—Burlington, Vermont

Blue Ridge Community College—Wyers Care, Virginia

Lord Fairfax Community College—Middleton, Virginia

Southern Junior Seminary—Buena Vista, Virginia

Virginia Intermont College—Bristol, Virginia

Virginia Polytechnic Institute—Blacksburg, Virginia

Washington State University—Pullman, Washington

Olympia Vocational Technical Institute, Olympia, Washington

West Virginia University—Morgantown, West Virginia

University of Wisconsin—River Falls, Wisconsin

Northwest Community College—Powell, Wyoming

Appendix IV

Colleges of veterinary medicine are located at the following institutions:

Auburn University
Auburn, Alabama 36830

University of California
Davis, California 95616

Colorado State University
Fort Collins, Colorado 80621

University of Georgia
Athens, Georgia 30601

University of Illinois
Urbana, Illinois 61801

Iowa State University
Ames, Iowa 50010

Kansas State University
Manhattan, Kansas 66502

Michigan State University
East Lansing, Michigan 48823

University of Minnesota
St. Paul, Minnesota 55101

University of Missouri
Columbia, Missouri 65202

Cornell University
Ithaca, New York 14850

Ohio State University
Columbus, Ohio 43210

Oklahoma State University
Stillwater, Oklahoma 74074

University of Guelph
Guelph, Ontario, Canada

University of Pennsylvania
Philadelphia, Pennsylvania 19104

Universite de Montreal
St.-Hyacinthe, Quebec, Canada

Purdue University
Lafayette, Indiana 47907

University of Saskatchewan
Saskatoon, Saskatchewan, Canada

Texas A&M University
College Station, Texas 77843

Tuskegee Institute
Tuskegee Institute, Alabama 36088

Washington State University
Pullman, Washington 99163

Index